Advance Praise for
COACHING FOR (A) CHANGE

"Greg Giuliano's *Coaching for (a) Change* is a masterful blend of insightful wisdom and practical coaching strategies. Greg's profound insights into the intricacies of effective coaching offer a refreshing perspective on engaging and empowering teams. His GR8 Coaching Framework is a practical, results-driven approach that transforms the way leaders interact with their teams. By focusing on trust, communication, and accountability, Greg provides a roadmap for creating a positive and productive organizational culture. This book is an invaluable resource for any leader looking to foster real change and drive their team to new heights of success."

—**DR. MARSHALL GOLDSMITH**,
Thinkers50 #1 Executive Coach and *New York Times*
bestselling author of *The Earned Life*, *Triggers*,
and *What Got You Here Won't Get You There*

"*Coaching for (a) Change: How to Engage, Empower, and Activate People* is an exceptional resource for anyone looking to elevate their coaching skills. Through the Be a GR8 Coach program, Greg and his team have helped to transform leadership in our organization, moving us from a command-and-control style to one that empowers and inspires our teams. The overwhelmingly positive response from across our organization is a testament to the program's effectiveness in driving performance and impact. This book is a must-read for anyone serious about becoming a better Leader and Coach."

—**JOHN MCKENNY**, Senior Vice President and General Manager, BMC, Intelligent Z Optimization and Transformation

"As someone who has experienced firsthand the transformative power of Dr. Greg Giuliano's coaching, I can confidently say *Coaching for (a) Change* is a game-changer for Leaders. Greg's approach enabled me to shift from a command-and-control style to one that truly engages and empowers my team. His GR8 Coaching Framework is practical and adaptable, making it possible for any Leader to foster a culture of ownership, innovation, and increased impact, not to mention having fun while driving outcomes! This book isn't just theory—it's an actionable guide that I return to repeatedly for its invaluable insights and tools. For anyone looking to elevate their leadership and drive real change, this book is a must-read and a must-do."

—**MAYA DILLON**, Head of Communications, US, HSBC

"Greg's work with our Leaders and teams helped us shift from managing to coaching and leading through change. His contribution has been invaluable. This book is a must for new and seasoned leaders alike."

—**CHRIS KAY**, SEVP, Consumer & Business Banking, Enterprise Platforms, M&T Bank

"Greg's coaching with our teams made us more effective and more aligned. We make decisions faster. People are more empowered. Our employee engagement jumped by double digits. His lessons are simple and straightforward. And he's put it all in this book."

—**AARTHI MURALI**, EVP, Fleet Management, Holman

"*Coaching for (a) Change* is a great read for anyone who wants to create a team and organization that values leadership, empowerment, and accountability. Greg Giuliano draws on his more than twenty years of experience to show how to be an effective Coach and truly empower people."

—**BRIAN SHERMAN**, Chief People Officer,
Delta Dental of California & Affiliates

"My job as a Leader is to make things better for the organization, my team, and each individual. *Coaching for (a) Change* is something I can go back to again and again to keep my skills fresh and to continually improve. I've been the recipient of Greg's wisdom and coaching for many years now and have always walked away more grounded, confident, and armed with practical approaches to problem-solving. Greg's coaching helps me set my teams up for success. Now I can share his book with the Leaders in my organization to help us all build a culture of coaching, empowerment, and trust."

—**CAROLYN HENRY**, VP/GM,
Americas Regional Marketing, Intel

"Greg is a force, and he's fun. Greg has been a trusted guide on my leadership journey, never pushing, always asking the right questions. He helps good Leaders and teams become better Leaders and teams. Like his other books, *Coaching for (a) Change* will become a gift I'll share with my Leaders to help them become the Coaches our people want."

—**TODD BURGER**, Chief Automotive Officer, AAA Mountain West Group

"When I read *Coaching for (a) Change*, I could hear Greg talking to me. His coaching and advice have never failed me. His book delivers too."

—**JANET WIDMANN**, Operating Partner, Varsity Healthcare Partners

"This should be required reading for first-time Leaders, long-time Leaders, and everyone in between. It's invaluable advice and terrific coaching in book form."

—**RICK WARREN**, CFO/COO, Innovation Care Partners

"The incomparable Greg Giuliano gifts us with a guide and game-changer for Managers of every level. Packed with practical coaching techniques, *Coaching for (a) Change* is essential for anyone wanting to drive team success and organizational growth!"

—**INGRID STABB**, AVP, Great Place to Work®, author of *The Career Within You*

"If you aspire to be a better Leader, take the lessons in *Coaching for (a) Change* to heart. Greg shares a powerful yet practical approach for shifting your thinking and, most importantly, your actions!"

—**JULIE PERSON**, Chief Administrative Officer, Third Harmonic Bio

"If you're looking for a radical, positive change to your work as a Manager, pick up *Coaching for (a) Change* and do the work. Start coaching your team and stop managing them—and watch your team's successes soar."

—**PHIL GERBYSHAK**, speaker, author, and podcaster, TheHappinessPractices.com

"In *Coaching for (a) Change*, Greg Giuliano reminds us that Leaders are disruptors who create the future. Delivering transformation at scale requires shifting from Expert Problem-Solver to Leader of people and authentic Coach. Greg provides an approachable, actionable way for Leaders to be the Coaches their teams want."

—**CHAD REESE**, VP, Marketing Operations, Cisco

COACHING FOR (A) CHANGE

HOW TO ENGAGE, EMPOWER, AND ACTIVATE PEOPLE

GREG GIULIANO

WREN HOUSE
press

COACHING FOR (A) CHANGE
How to Engage, Empower, and Activate People
First Edition

ISBN   979-8-9912039-2-0   *Hardcover*
        979-8-9912039-1-3   *Paperback*
        979-8-9912039-0-6   *Ebook*

For Duke—Mentor, Coach, Friend.

STEVE "DUKE" SHIPLEY (1947–2023)

People come into our lives, and we are changed. I know this to be true because of Steve Shipley. Meeting Duke changed the trajectory of my life. He was a mentor, Coach, and friend for over twenty-five years.

He was a gifted leader, and one of the kindest, most generous, funniest, smartest, and wisest people I've ever known. It's on me to be worthy of the gifts he shared with me over the years and pay it forward. David Whyte's poem "Sweet Darkness" ends, "Anything or anyone that doesn't bring you alive is too small for you." Everyone who knew Steve Shipley was brought alive. He was big enough for all of us. He made us all better. Thanks, Duke!

Serve to Lead

—MOTTO, ROYAL MILITARY
ACADEMY SANDHURST

CONTENTS

FOREWORD

by Farren Drury MBE

WHY GREG GIULIANO?

Greg and I did our International Coach Federation (ICF) certification training together nearly twenty years ago. I had served twenty-three years as a British army officer, and I understood command and control. I had learned to embrace "serve to lead" as a truly powerful philosophy of leadership, how I could bring my soldiers with me, to win their loyalty and trust—by serving them. Command and control, however, was still very much the way to lead, and I took that responsibility very seriously—on occasions to the detriment of my own health and well-being, and often counter to fully engaging, trusting, and releasing the full potential of my soldiers.

I left the army, having adopted two children, and I was on a steep learning curve. Learning how to coach was part of that transformational journey, and together we were learning how challenging it was to make the change to a coaching approach. We, like everyone we knew, had been brought up in a world in which people love to tell others what to do, to give their advice—parents, grandparents, teachers, lecturers, bosses, friends, colleagues—and we followed suit. The shift wasn't easy, and it took effort.

Greg had a natural instinct from the start. As three directors of five of our Global Leadership businesses, we were doing a triad coaching session—Greg was coaching me, and Alan was observing.

Greg listened intently, recognising the work ethic I had always prided myself on, and asked me a question that changed everything for me:

"So...what are you doing it all for, Farren?"

OMG—I stopped, I cried (we all cried—true empathy among three experienced Leaders), and I said, "I'm doing it to make my mum proud."

"Don't you get it, Farren..." (Pause...more tears!)

"What?" I asked.

"She's already proud of you," said Greg.

A moment in time, a liberation, a weight off my shoulders, a realisation. Thank you, Greg. My mother had died some seven years before, and in that moment, in that one transformational question, Greg had released me to lead a different life!

WHY THIS BOOK?

Not every coaching interaction will be like that! What Greg offers in this outstanding book is the opportunity for every Leader (see list above: parents, bosses, etc.) to engage with people in a different way. Coaching questions demand curiosity and belief in the potential of the person you're asking to think for themselves and to use their brains to work out the optimal approach to solving a problem, taking an opportunity, and making things better. Neuroscience tells us that trusting another engenders trustworthiness. Coaching generates win-win scenarios, and in this book, Greg superbly presents how we can find more and more such life-enhancing moments.

Offering guidance, evidence, and enlightenment, Greg brings powerful stories from business, sports, and life to demonstrate the case for change. He succinctly brings us the essence of what other great Leaders, authors, and researchers have studied, experienced, and shifted to give you confidence you can make this change too. Use the excellent models he's designed, the approach he offers, and the inspiring benefits he's witnessed, and you, too, can secure impacts on your life and work that you can only now imagine.

WHY NOW?

In this age of instant communication, data overload, and increasing demands on Leaders and their teams to be more productive, to meet deadlines, and to bring innovation—all whilst often working remotely—empowerment, engagement, and trust are essential to success. You can't do it all yourself. You will burn out, and your people will stagnate or leave. You must bring your team(s) with you, empower them to think for themselves, and trust them to take action to reach the vision/mission you have given them or cocreated with them. No matter how good your idea or concept is to get things done, execution of the task will never be as good as it could have been had you collaborated and engaged your people in designing the way and then releasing them to complete the task. Your role is to set them up for success—not do their job for them.

Greg is again at the zeitgeist—he sees what Leaders and their people need today, and he makes it easier for you to adopt this empowering approach and make (a) change. Enjoy the ride!

* * *

A personal note about Farren. He is a true Ultra Leader, always empathetic and compassionate, always exploring ways to learn, grow, and be of service to others. I'm honored he agreed to share his thoughts in the Foreword to this book.

Farren had a distinguished military career, winning the Commando Medal while with the Royal Marines. He was awarded the MBE for services to the former Yugoslavia. He also received the Wilkinson Sword of Peace during the peace process in Northern Ireland on behalf of the infantry battalion he commanded.

I've known Farren for almost twenty years. Whenever I am with Farren, I laugh, I learn, and I am stretched to be better. His passion and enthusiasm are palpable and infectious. As a Leader and Coach, he has a determination to make a positive and sustainable difference in society. He is the founder of an amazing organization: Make It Yours (gomakeityours.com).

—Greg

INTRODUCTION

DON'T LIKE BEING TOLD WHAT TO DO. I NEVER HAVE. And yet there I was, in my first "leadership" role, taking orders—and giving orders—all day long.

I had no prior leadership experience, just some ideas I'd picked up from a management book or two. Without any other template or basis for practice, I took all my cues from my boss, who, like the majority of leaders at our company, followed the command-and-control model of leadership. He told me what to do, I listened, and then I turned around and told my team what to do.

It didn't work.

Early on in my tenure, my team was assigned a particularly challenging project. We had been tasked with staffing a community outreach experience that would take place over two weeks right before Christmas. There were lots of moving parts, including engaging volunteers to participate throughout the two weeks. Doing what I thought I was supposed to, I looked at the project and assigned each team member a specific set of responsibilities.

One of my team members didn't like his assignment. I'd asked him to take charge of engaging the volunteers over the course of the project. "That's not my responsibility," he said. "I don't agree that I should be doing that."

I don't remember exactly how I responded, but the gist of it was, "Tough. You're doing it anyway."

I wasn't trying to be mean. I was just doing what I believed was expected of me. Plus, I like to move to action quickly, and I figured the best way to get to action in this case was to dictate exactly how he was going to do his job.

He didn't see it that way. Instead, he dug in. "I am not doing this," he said. "And if this is what you're going to have me do, I guess I don't want to be on this team anymore."

Stupidly, I replied, "Yeah, I guess you don't."

Soon after, he quit the company.

That was our loss. He was a talented guy, and all I had to do to keep him around was to listen to him, engage him, and work with him to find a solution. But I didn't. Instead, I treated him in a way that I would never want to be treated myself. If I were in his shoes, I would have quit too.

The team member's departure wasn't just a humbling experience for me. It put the whole team in a bind. Now, not only did we have to complete our project, but we had to do it shorthanded. Meanwhile, I had the unenviable job of taking on our departed team member's workload while searching for his replacement.

What a headache. Something had to change.

If I wanted to bring lasting positive change to my organization, I needed to change my entire philosophy of leadership—and fast. I needed to turn things upside down.

HUMANS AREN'T RESOURCES

After my early leadership blunder, I came to a realization that would change the entire trajectory of my career: command and control doesn't work. Why? Because people are not assets. People are not resources. People are not capital. People are people.

The people on your team aren't resources to be managed or capital to be spent. They are skilled contributors who want to be led.

Effective Leaders engage, empower, and activate the teams they lead. But you can't do that if you're dictating your team's work to them. Sure, you might get the results you want in the short term, but that success has a shelf life. When your leadership strategy is centered around getting your team members to comply, eventually those team members will check out—or in my case, leave.

Today, this idea is well-established. In the late 1990s, however, it had just begun to take root when thought leaders like Ken Blanchard, Spencer Johnson, and Tom Peters all started banging the drum of employee engagement. Why? Because, as Daniel Pink would later say in his book *Drive*, "People want a sense of autonomy. They want to be able to demonstrate mastery, and they want to know that the work they're doing is meaningful and purposeful work. They want to be connected to something important."[1]

This wasn't just feel-good rhetoric to help make employees happier at work. Already, the move to digital, remote, and asynchronous work was underway, and forward-thinking leaders like Pink saw the writing on the wall. To create positive change in these modern workspaces, Leaders would have to trust their team members to work on their own with little intervention.

Of course, with this need to change came a host of questions:

- How do you lead when you often only see your team during meetings?
- How do you ensure that your team members understand their responsibilities and are executing them to the best of their abilities?
- How do you make sure your team members are doing what they're supposed to without micromanaging their every decision?

---

1   Daniel Pink, *Drive: The Surprising Truth About What Motivates Us* (New York: Riverhead Books, 2009).

The answer: By remembering to serve to lead. And to serve, coach.

THE CASE FOR COACHING

Great Leaders engage and empower their teams, set the tone for how people interact, and guide their team members to effectively deliver on their objectives. This is how Leaders serve their teams. Companies that adopt a coaching-based model have more engaged teams, generate higher output, and generally outperform their competitors. Research backs this up:

- Companies that integrate coaching report a median return on investment of over 700 percent, according to the International Coaching Federation (ICF).[2]
- Organizations that successfully engage their employees achieve earnings-per-share growth over four times higher than their competitors, according to Gallup.[3]
- High-performing organizations are more than twice as likely to have strong coaching cultures, which leads to

2   International Coach Federation, *ICF Global Coaching Client Study: Executive Summary*, 2009, https://researchportal.coachingfederation.org/Document/Pdf/190.pdf.
3   Gallup, *State of the American Workplace: Employee Engagement Insights for U.S. Business Leaders*, 2013, https://mediaassets.kjrh.com/html/pdfs/unhappyemployees_gallup.pdf.

higher engagement and motivation, according to the
Human Capital Institute and the ICF.[4]

There is a direct correlation between employee engagement and Managers who exhibit the traits of a good Coach—
that is, Managers who care about their team, who coach
their team, and who provide regular feedback tend to have
more engaged and high-functioning teams, according to the
Institute for Leadership and Management.

But why? How is it that coaching your teams can lead to
such outsized results?

It all comes down to trust.

As David Kingsley, the chief people officer at Illumio, said
when I was interviewing him for my *Ultra Leadership* podcast,
the three most powerful words a Leader
can utter are "I trust you."[5] Trust sets
your team on fire. Command and control
extinguishes that fire. It's disempowering. It's demotivating. It's boring. After all,

**The three most
powerful words a
Leader can utter
are "I trust you."**

why bother going above and beyond when I can't trust my
Leader to have my back?

---

4   Barbara A. Trautlein, J. Matthew Becker, and Shawna Corden, *Building a
     Coaching Culture for Change Management*, accessed July 2, 2024, https://
     www.hci.org/webcast/building-coaching-culture-change-management.
5   Greg Giuliano, *Ultra Leadership*, podcast, "The 3 Most Powerful Words in
     Leadership with David Kingsley," Apple Podcasts, June 5, 2024, https://
     podcasts.apple.com/us/podcast/the-3-most-powerful-words-in-leadership-
     with-david-kingsley/id1643988354?i=1000657880175.

Because, as they say in the business world: people don't quit bad jobs; they quit bad Managers. If people like their work but can't stand their boss, they'll leave for a similar job without the drama.

That's precisely what happened to me the first time I stepped into a leadership role. Quickly I learned that if I didn't want to keep losing good people, I had to change my approach. Once I ditched the command-and-control mindset and tried coaching for a change, I became a trusted resource who was there to keep my team moving forward.

When someone hit a wall, I didn't solve their problem for them or dictate what they should do. I walked them through the problem so they could arrive at the best solution on their own. As a result, not only did I help my team deliver their best work, but I was able to drive positive change for my organization. The best part, however, was how making this shift deepened the trust between my team and me and extended that trust between team members. As our trust in one another grew, we were able to level up both as a team and as individuals.

And here's the best part: if I could make this change, anyone could. Even a basic understanding of coaching principles and best practices can help you engage your team and drive better results. In this book, I'll teach you everything you need to get started.

COACHING ISN'T THE END—
IT'S THE MEANS TO THE END

If there's one thing I've learned about coaching over the past thirty years, it's that getting better at it is a lifelong pursuit. When I was just starting out, I wasn't much of a Coach at all; I showed up to a meeting, we had a nice cup of coffee, we enjoyed some nice conversation, and that was that. No discussion of next steps, no deadlines, and no accountability. I had been a therapist. How hard could this coaching thing be?

Since then, I've learned a lot. My career has taken a few interesting twists and turns—I began in academia, spent some time in corporate, became a therapist, then became a Coach and consultant. For over twenty years, I have run my own coaching and consulting companies, where we engage organizations by working with high-level executives and their teams using modern leadership principles and tools to enable positive transformation.

When starting out, many think they're good Coaches when, in reality, they're just good at chitchat. That's not what coaching is all about. Coaching is a means to an end; it's not the end. Coaching should engage a person and empower them to achieve their stated goals. To become a more effective Coach, I needed a better system. Over the years, I found that certain questions helped me to help the person I was coaching focus on their desired outcome, examine the current reality, map the way forward, and take action to achieve their goals. The questions I've relied upon became the GR8 Coaching Framework outlined in this book.

All these years in, the framework still helps me to keep my conversations on track and my clients moving forward to their goals. If a client shows up and doesn't know what they want to talk about, I start from the top: What's going on? What's the best possible outcome? What's in your way?

Through questions like these, the GR8 Coaching Framework has helped numerous Leaders shift their cultures toward greater engagement and empowerment by coaching more and commanding less.

I have faith in the model because it works. The viability of my company depends on engagement, empowerment, and creative problem-solving. We don't just teach what you'll discover in this book. We use it. Why? To engage our clients with integrity, we have to walk the walk. And a number of the people on our team are experienced independent contractors who do not need to be told what to do. We are all open to being coached by one another. If I treated any of the professionals working with me today like I treated my team member thirty-plus years ago, the very talented people I work with would tell me to get lost. Instead, I've had the honor and privilege of working with the people on my team for years.

In these ways, coaching continues to yield value both within my business and for my clients. I've tested and perfected the coaching principles, mindsets, and practices you'll find in this book, and I know they will help you too, whether you've recently pivoted toward coaching or you're a seasoned and experienced Coach looking to sharpen the saw.

I have shared some of what I've learned in my earlier books: *The Hero's Journey* (2014), *Ultra Leadership* (2016), and *The Next Normal* (2022). Each of these books focuses on a particular aspect of leadership and change to help Leaders sharpen their skills in a range of applications. But while both *Ultra Leadership* and *The Next Normal* in particular explored aspects of coaching, here in this book we'll take a deep dive into the mindset, skills, and best practices of effective coaching in a changing world.

A ROADMAP FOR SUCCESS

This book will help you build the mindset and skill set of an effective Coach for your team. To help you on that journey, I have divided this book into two parts.

- Part One: From Manager to Coach. Coaching begins with a particular mindset and depends on a distinct skill set. You must believe that the person in front of you has the answer in them, that they are capable and can do what the organization expects them to do. Your goal isn't to solve their problems but rather to empower them and encourage them to grow. In this section, we will explore the core concepts and practices of an effective Coach.

- **Part Two: Be a GR8 Coach.** In this section, I introduce the GR8 Coaching Framework, the GR8 1:1s Framework, and other tools to help you make the shift from Manager to Coach. These are the tools that I reach for to lead any coaching conversation—individual coaching, 1:1s, team meetings, and everything in between—because they are the most effective tools in my toolkit. These frameworks and tools include intentional, open-ended questions designed to put the onus and ownership on your team members so they can consistently solve their own problems and advocate for themselves.

When our team engages clients to teach the GR8 Coaching Framework during our coaching programs, we consistently see Leaders coming to the same realization I did: they thought they were coaching, but really, they were either still dictating or asking leading questions designed to help their team members arrive at their solution.

The questions in the GR8 Coaching Framework and GR8 1:1s Framework are designed to move you from problem-solving mode into coaching mode. With little or no practice, these questions will help you move your team members from an idea into an exploration of their current state, careful consideration of a variety of options, and aligned and purposeful action. The process gets everyone to slow down, explore different possibilities, and find the best solution that leads to the best results.

That last point is important. To harness our creativity and drive true innovation, we must be willing to survey the field and find new ways of working and problem-solving. Otherwise, we're just doing what C. Otto Scharmer, author of *Theory U*, calls "downloading," using old methods to address new situations. That's the antithesis of creativity and innovation—and the antithesis of what makes a Great Coach.

According to the International Coaching Federation, a key to successful coaching is establishing a contract for completion. Instead of just talking about a goal, you and your coachee reach an agreement about what moving forward looks like. From there, your job is to play accountability partner, holding them to what they're doing next and when they're going to do it.

This is what makes the GR8 Coaching Framework different from other coaching models I have seen, and why it's so effective: it provides a concrete, repeatable system to listen well, ask great questions, and help you and your team keep moving forward and creating value for your organization.

YOU GO FIRST

It all starts with you. To become a Great Coach, you must first be coachable yourself. Are you willing to learn and try new things? Are you open to new experiences, receptive to feedback, and willing to learn and change? Do you exhibit what thought leader and author Carol Dweck refers to as a "growth mindset"?

Coaches, like the best Leaders, are adaptable, open to learning, developing, and growing. In many cases, insight leads directly to action. We learn something new. We think "aha!" and we behave differently.

Often, though, we need a little help making the change, even if we want to. Habits are habits. But when my own coaching clients begin asking the questions in the GR8 Coaching Framework, they're shocked by how effective it is in helping them to break old habits. No longer tempted to jump in and solve their team's problems, they're able to lead their team toward understanding their challenges, solving problems creatively, and owning the result. Just by following the script, they make more progress in fifteen minutes than they had been able to make in fifteen weeks!

It really can be that easy—but you have to be willing to do the work and learn from the results.

To that point, this is a "roll up your sleeves and practice" kind of book. Be ready to try out the concepts I discuss here. You won't get much value by simply reading the book, setting it down, and forgetting about it. So, get busy, get active, and practice the three Ts of learning: thinking, talking, and testing. Think about the concepts in this book. Talk through your insights with others. Finally, test these ideas with your team. You'll get much more value from this book—and much

more insight into how you operate as a Leader and a Coach—
through direct action.

I'm not here to waste your time or show you how smart
I am. I'm here to give you simple frameworks and tools that
will help you become a better Leader by becoming a better
Coach. That said, as you move through this book, you may
not see the value of the GR8 Coaching Framework right away.
If you find that's the case, here's my suggestion: try it anyway.
Use the GR8 Coaching Framework during your next team
meeting and see what you learn. You don't need to be perfect.
Just get started and learn as you go. It's like a very old cereal
commercial, "Try it. You'll like it." As I said earlier, insight can
follow action.

I'm inviting you to go on a journey with the intention that,
by trying coaching for a change, you will change too. And
as you change, so will those around you—your team, your
fellow Leaders, even your entire organization. If you're ready
for that kind of radical, positive change, then let's get started.

PART ONE

FROM MANAGER TO COACH

To understand what makes a Great Coach, first, we need to understand the difference between a Manager and a Leader. A Manager runs processes: do what we did yesterday, but a little more efficiently and a little bit faster today. A Leader, on the other hand, focuses on creating nonincremental change. A Leader wants to increase their contribution to the organization by making some *thing* or *experience* different and better, by making their team different and better, and by making each team member different and better.

As I said in *Ultra Leadership*, leadership enables positive transformation. The same goes for coaching. If you can encourage and accelerate positive transformation with your team, you will create positive transformation for your entire organization.

Leadership enables positive transformation.

Like many aspiring Leaders, you may find this mindset shift from Manager to Coach to be a tricky one to make. After all, you likely reached your current role because you were a good doer and an excellent problem-solver. But now that you're in a leadership position, it's not your job to be a doer or a problem-solver anymore. Instead, it's your job to empower others to be the doers and problem-solvers, to believe that they have the ability, knowledge, skill, and experience to solve the problems that face them.

If you're focused on solving everyone's problems, you'll only ever be effective in the narrow band of your own vocational skill set. If you rose through the ranks as an engineer, for

instance, you'll only ever be able to solve engineering problems as the Chief Doer and Expert Problem-Solver. However,
by developing your skills as a Coach, you will extend your
impact beyond your current vocational expertise.

That is, as long as you follow a clear process. Here in
Part One, I will show you how to shift your mindset from Manager to Coach. Rather than approaching your role through the
lens of Chief Doer and Expert Problem-Solver, you will learn
to embrace your role as an Aligner and Facilitator of Change.

1

THE CHANGING
WORK OF
LEADERSHIP

THE RESULTS ARE IN: THE OLD LEADERSHIP MOD-
els no longer apply. It's beyond time we change how
we lead people and teams.

It's already happening. According to a study published by *Harvard Business Review*, the role of managers is
evolving. Whereas leadership roles used to rely on the traditional command-and-control model, today's increasingly
digitized, remote, or hybrid organizations are looking for
collaborators, facilitators, and Coaches.[6]

6   Brian Kropp, Alexia Cambon, and Sara Clark, "What Does It Mean to Be...

One Coach you might be familiar with inhabits this new role—Ted Lasso. In the television series of the same name, Ted knows *he* can't win the soccer match for his team. Only the players can win *for themselves*. No amount of commanding can determine the outcome—only smart execution of the strategy by engaged and empowered players. This is a good thing for Coach Lasso because, as the show explores to such great comedic effect, he doesn't know all that much about soccer. Before joining AFC Richmond, he coached *American* football!

Like Ted Lasso, Coaches in the real world create the conditions for their teams to perform their core work. Then, during timeouts, the Coach offers targeted support and guidance, whether to the entire team or through 1:1s and check-ins. The Coach shapes the strategy and works to bring out the best in every player so that they can work together to achieve the team's shared goal.

The same applies to business today. If I am your Leader, I can't—and shouldn't—do your work for you. I can only be effective if I provide coaching to help you improve and make sure everyone works together in a coordinated way.

Why? Because the command-and-control approach to leadership doesn't make sense in today's world. It may be cliché at this point to say it, but change is a constant now. There

---

...a Manager Today?," *Harvard Business Review*, April 15, 2021, https://hbr.org/2021/04/what-does-it-mean-to-be-a-manager-today.

is no going back. Whereas the traditional hierarchical model dominated the twentieth century, today's organizations are often flatter and more matrixed. Shared workspaces, hybrid work, and fully remote work are becoming increasingly common. These changes necessitate asynchronous communications, so the Manager–employee relationship isn't the same as it was when everyone was always in the same building at the same time. This shift, along with significant technological shifts and a new generation of workers with different expectations, has profoundly changed the way we work. Today, you simply can't "walk the floor" to check up on people—you have to trust them to do the work on their own.

Fortunately, within this changing, sometimes uncertain environment, there is also opportunity. If a strong ship is seaworthy, then a strong organization is change-worthy. To be change-worthy, today's flatter, more matrixed organizations must embrace a new kind of Leader, someone who can steer their teams into change and lead without fear.

The ever-increasing need to steer into change requires more and more organizations to set aside the command-and-control model and instead prioritize a way of leading people and teams where Leaders create the conditions for their workers to engage, feel like they belong, and bring their full, best selves to work. In such an environment, team members feel empowered to do what needs to be done on behalf of the team and the organization—whether in person, through a video call, or through asynchronous work.

It all starts with the key characteristics of the new modern Leader. Let's explore what that looks like.

TODAY'S LEADERSHIP DEFINED

Today's Leaders must evolve into what I call *Ultra Leaders*. Drawing from my experiences as an ultramarathon runner, I coined this term to describe how this transformation occurs. The premise goes something like this: The word *ultra* means "beyond usual and ordinary." Ultramarathons, then, are beyond usual and ordinary. You're going "above and beyond" the usual marathon distance—and in so doing, pushing your body above and beyond what it's accustomed to.

Usual and ordinary leadership seeks stasis, is uncomfortable with uncertainty, lacks curiosity, and relies on title or position rather than on relationships to drive results. Ultra Leadership pushes the limits, disrupts the status quo, understands the needs of others, and builds relationships to engage others and drive positive change. It's about moving an organization or a project from point A to point B. It's about creating high-performing teams to join in that work. Finally, it's about helping individuals move from good to better. In this sense, the work of the Ultra Leader is to enable positive transformation, to change reality, to

Ultra Leadership pushes the limits, disrupts the status quo, understands the needs of others, and builds relationships to engage others and drive positive change.

create the conditions for the organization, its teams, and its people to go above and beyond, over and over again.

Fortunately, the way of the Ultra Leader isn't rocket science. It's as easy as A, B, C and 1-2-3.

A, B, C AND 1-2-3

To be an Ultra Leader—and a Great Coach—you'll need a strong foundation, including the ABCs of Leadership: Aligning people, Building bench strength, and Coordinating action. You'll also need a system such as the three-part team leadership and team operating system for engaging, empowering, and activating people that I introduced in *The Next Normal*. Remembering your ABCs and implementing this 1-2-3 team operating system can help you become a great Leader and make the first steps toward becoming a Great Coach. For the rest of the chapter, we'll explore each of these ABCs one by one, along with the 1-2-3s that follow.

A: Align People

The first fundamental job of a Leader is aligning people around what's most important. In centuries past, before the advent of GPS, navigators would use the stars to guide them. As long as they understood their position relative to these stars, they knew they were on the right course.

Most organizations have guiding stars as well in the form of their mission, vision, and values. These guiding stars help

drive decision-making within the organization and determine how different teams will use the time, energy, and
resources available to them.

Effective teams keep those guiding stars in sight at all
times so that they can make decisions that align with the
organization's goals.

As a Leader, your job is to align people around your guiding stars. An aligned team knows the answers to questions
like these:

- What is the organizational vision?
- What is the organization's strategy?
- What is this team's unique mission in support of the
  vision and strategy?
- What is my role and responsibility?
- How are we measuring success?

Ultra Leaders articulate their team's mission to create
shared clarity and alignment. Once they're confident everyone is aligned, they turn their teams loose to shape their work
and achieve their best.

Unfortunately, failure to create this kind of basic alignment is all too common in large organizations. I have seen
this firsthand. In one organization I was working with, one
team was charged with reducing expenses for the company, while a second team was told that the organization
intended to grow as rapidly as possible and that they would

spare no expense in that pursuit. The two teams' goals were at odds: how could the first team possibly manage expenses successfully if another team was empowered to spend however it saw fit? They couldn't—at least, not without coordinating their efforts. Unfortunately, neither team knew of the other's priorities, leading them to unwittingly compete against each other.

This misalignment created a ripple effect across the entire organization, affecting the work of nearly every department. Leadership knew they had a problem, but they couldn't identify the cause. When our company engaged with them, we were able to help them (1) figure out the problem, (2) define success as an organization, and then (3) align their teams around that shared vision of success. However, all of this could have been avoided if leadership had been more intentional about communicating their vision and creating alignment in the first place.

As this organization learned, effective alignment is twofold, involving alignment within teams and alignment between and among teams. As their operating model began to shift to encourage this horizontal communication, these teams were able to reduce conflicts and the duplication of work. More importantly, by opening conversations and creating alignment, the organization was able to identify ways the organization could have its cake and eat it too—that is, achieve growth and manage expenses.

B: Build Bench Strength

Ultra Leaders work to make their team and each team member better. By developing individual and collective capacity, they build bench strength. Building team bench strength, collective capacity, begins with setting some basic behavioral expectations:

- How will we treat one another?
- How will we communicate with one another?
- What can partners, stakeholders, and customers expect from us consistently?

With those basics in place, you set your team up for greatness. You create an environment where people learn to trust one another, cooperate, and collaborate. (There's a detailed agenda for convening this type of team commitments conversation in *The Next Normal*.)

This is precisely what Head Coach Steve Kerr did during the Golden State Warriors' historic run between 2014 and 2019. Coach Kerr set clear behavioral expectations for how the team would work together to achieve its objective. First, he defined what high performance looked like for the team, and then he worked with individual players to understand their roles and how they could meet those expectations. Often, this meant providing direct feedback on their performance and what they could work on next—whether it was getting in position quicker, making certain shots, or communicating better on-court.

Chief among Coach Kerr's expectations was frequent and candid communication. The team wouldn't get better unless they learned together. Of course, good communication doesn't amount to much without effective application. That's why the Warriors also practiced what they preached—a lot. In fact, one time at a press conference after a game his team had won, Coach Kerr commented that the win was ugly and that his team did not perform at their peak. When pressed by a reporter for a reason for the poor performance, Coach Kerr responded, "We stopped talking to one another."

Kerr doesn't just focus on team capacity. He works to make every member of the team a better person and better player. Ultra Leaders get to know their team members as individuals because each one of them has individual needs.

"My job is to understand the circumstances of every single player on the team," said Kerr. "[I want to] connect with them. Compassion is one of our core values...you have to have it to understand everybody's got difficulties in their lives, adversity, and that you've got to help them through it."[7]

Your role as Leader of a team is to develop each team member. Seek to understand them. Demonstrate real concern for them. What do they want to get better at? What do they need to get better at to succeed in their current role and

---

7   Nick McCarvel, "Coach Steve Kerr: The Greatest Athletes Aren't Afraid of Failure," Olympics.com, April 28, 2021, https://olympics.com/en/news/steve-kerr-steph-curry-greatest-athletes-nba-usa-basketball.

accelerate their path to their next role? That's part of the job. Make people better.

C: Coordinate Action

In our current business environment, work is often asynchronous, individuals often work remotely, and people are spread across geography and time zones. You might go days without seeing one of your direct reports or team members. In fact, I know many teams that only meet in person once or twice a year. For this reason, Ultra Leaders must coordinate action so that their team members feel empowered and accountable to independently make decisions aligned with the mission, goals, and priorities of their key stakeholders.

With your team aligned around its important work, it's on you to ensure ongoing follow-up and follow-through with tracking and adjustment mechanisms to ensure that all your team's plates keep spinning. When you set team practices, rituals, and routines to coordinate action, you empower each person to set their near-term deliverables and development goals, keeping the team's work on track. Each team member must understand what their work is, whether they're working on the right stuff at the right time, how their work relates to the team and company's larger goals, and how they are accountable for their work.

How do you achieve all that? When you follow the ABCs, you create a culture of trust. Ultra Leaders trust that their team's decisions align with both the team's and the organization's priorities. Team members trust that their team leader is invested in developing them. You and your team work in a system that is transparent and inclusive. Everyone knows who's doing what and by when.

EASY AS 1-2-3

Conceptually, the ABCs of Leadership are easy to understand. As you were reading the previous section, you probably thought, *Well, duh.*

Putting the ABCs into practice in a simple, repeatable, and scalable way, however, requires some scaffolding. To that end, we developed a three-legged stool that provides just such a system for Aligning people, Building bench strength, and Coordinating action. Using this system, Ultra Leaders create teams that don't need Managers. Instead, they create teams that want Coaches.

It's as easy as 1-2-3:

1. Team Roadmaps
2. Individual Tactical Action Plans (TAPs)
3. Coach First, Tell Last

Roadmaps, TAPs, and regular coaching bring the ABCs of Leadership to life. With Team Roadmaps and TAPs, you're Aligning people and Coordinating action. Through regular coaching focused on TAPs, you're Building bench strength. The Leaders and teams using this system experience higher engagement, greater empowerment, and successful activation to achieve their shared goals. Let's look at each element.

1: Team Roadmaps

The Team Roadmap is the simplest tool and process I've seen for keeping a team aligned.

The Team Roadmap aligns teams around their guiding stars. These guiding stars include vision, mission, strategy, execution plan, roles, accountabilities, and success measures. When completed, the Team Roadmap is a "plan on a page," indicating your mission, your success measures (outcomes and metrics), your "big rocks" (the work, projects, and initiatives you'll undertake to deliver your outcomes), and your workstream stewards (the team members who will organize the work, guide the people, and report on progress). If anyone should forget the team's mission or where the team is going, all they would need to do is to look at the Team Roadmap to jog their memory. The following page shows what the Team Roadmap looks like.

Every year at our company, we create a roadmap that aligns the team around our mission, describing the outcomes for the year and the work necessary to achieve those outcomes (the actions/"big rocks"). Then, we designate roles among team members, including who will act as a steward for different actions along the way.

TEAM ROADMAP

Mission:								Success Measures	
Stewards			Actions/Big Rocks (6 max)					Outcomes	Metrics

Team Roadmaps empower people to shape their work. A team member can use the Team Roadmap as a focusing point to see the work that belongs to them. The clear priorities articulated in the Team Roadmap enable team members to shape their work, quarter by quarter, in service of the team's shared goals.

In that way, the Team Roadmap is a tool for Aligning people. It's also a process to ensure sustained alignment. Alignment isn't the default setting for any team. It is the work of leadership to keep people aligned, so establish a good cadence to review your team's progress toward executing its Team Roadmap. Some teams convene a monthly review meeting. Some look at a workstream a week. I use a RAG (red, amber, green) system to report on the status of each big rock and outcome.

2: Tactical Action Plans

The second leg of our three-legged stool is the individual Tactical Action Plan (TAP).

TAPs are attention management tools that empower team members to shape their work and focus their development every ninety days. TAPs also ensure alignment, greater focus, and accountability while empowering each team member and creating psychological safety.

With the Team Roadmap as a guide, each member of your team can create their own Tactical Action Plan each quarter. The following page shows what the TAP looks like.

The TAP is divided into the following sections:

Outcomes

When I'm working with someone to create their TAP, 1 ask, "Of all the things on your plate that you believe are important, urgent, and yours to handle, which four are most important and most urgent?" Those four things go onto the TAP. These are the outcomes this person is accountable for delivering. They cannot be delegated or delayed.

Actions

"What must you do to achieve each outcome?" The objective is to get clear on what must happen in order to take positive steps toward each outcome.

1 like to keep this section simple. List no more than four tasks or actions for each outcome. This enables you to stay

TACTICAL ACTION PLAN

Name:				Quarter:
ACTIONS: (What must happen to achieve each Outcome?)				MY OUTCOMES: (What will you focus on delivering?)
				Business/People Objectives 1.
				2.
				3.
				4.
				MY DEVELOPMENT GOALS 1.
				2.

laser-focused on outcomes and to prioritize how you'll use your time, energy, and resources in the next ninety days.

Development Goals

Because you're always building bench strength (including your own), the TAP always includes development goals. To get started, I will ask two questions:

- To deliver your outcomes, succeed in your role, and accelerate your path to your next role, what do you want or need to get better at?
- What are the two most important development areas you want to focus on in the next ninety days?

Then, once clear development goals have been established, I ask, "What will you do to work on each development goal?" The goal of this question is to get team members to think in terms of education, experience, and exposure. For example, is it reading or listening to a podcast? Maybe it's working with a Coach. Maybe it's shadowing another Leader or executive.

Development goals could also be personal, like becoming more resilient or physically fit. Perhaps you'll set an exercise routine or start a meditation practice. You might pick a leadership goal, like getting better at delegating and coaching. Again, enter no more than four actions that represent the new practices, routines, or rituals you'll engage in to achieve each development goal.

3: Coach First, Tell Last

So now what do you do? Your team doesn't need you to tell them what to do. They know what to do. They've shaped their work using the guiding stars laid out in front of them. They don't need you to solve their problems for them. They own their situation, and they own their solutions.

SOME FREE ADVICE ON TAPS

Most of the Leaders and people I encounter complain that their calendars are out of control. They're in back-to-back meetings almost every day with no spare time. Sound familiar? If you're a Leader, I'll bet you a cup of coffee that if I look at your calendar today, I'd find that at least 20 percent of the meetings and tasks on your calendar belong to one of your direct reports. You are doing someone else's work. Which means you're not doing your work.

The TAP is a life-changing tool for the Leaders and people who use it. With your TAP in hand, look at your calendar and begin scrubbing. If there are meetings and tasks on your calendar that don't line up with your TAP, delegate them or delete them. Do this exercise every month or whenever you notice your calendar has once again mysteriously become populated with someone else's work.

When you and your team members have created and agreed on an individual TAP for each quarter, the TAP becomes a promise of accountability for them and a tool for you to Coordinate action and provide support. Use the TAP as a focal point for your 1:1s, ensuring you and your team members are making the most of each conversation, which brings us to the third leg of the stool.

They do need you to say, "I trust you." They do need you to be available to coach them and provide feedback when they get stuck. Otherwise, get out of the way.

That's what the third leg of the stool is for—helping you shift from Chief Doer and Expert Problem-Solver to Great Coach. Fight the urge to tell people what to do—and make engaging as a Coach your first instinct. When you act as a Coach, embracing the ABCs, you're engaging and empowering people. Empowered people don't need to or want to be told what to do, but they are open to coaching. Through coaching, you activate people to deliver business results while supporting their ongoing development to better themselves and up their performance.

Fight the urge to tell people what to do—and make engaging as a Coach your first instinct.

Shifting from Chief Doer and Expert Problem-Solver to Great Coach will give you back space and time. This is a big benefit. I know Leaders who still believe they need to have weekly 1:1s with every member of their team. How many hours have you spent in unproductive weekly 1:1 meetings? If you're anything like me, probably more than you'd like to admit.

As a Great Coach, you can change that. The mandatory weekly 1:1 is a relic of the command-and-control model. You don't need to do it—just like you don't need to walk the floor and talk to every member of your team every day. In an increasingly hybrid workplace with a dispersed workforce, not only are these old structures obsolete, but they're also impractical.

For example, say that you have twelve people on your team, or some crazy number like that. With your new coaching glasses on, you can easily see what each of those people has signed up to do for the quarter. It's on their TAP. You trust them to execute, and you make sure they know where they can find you if they run into a problem that's either too big for them or that they need to think through out loud. Knowing all this, is it worth your time to spend twelve hours or more a week on your 1:1s if no one needs them?

Sure, you may have one or two newer team members who want or need those regular check-ins. But most likely, you'll have other team members who only need a check-in once or twice a quarter. When you're a Coach, your team members set the cadence for 1:1s. You're just there to support them however they need it. After all, these meetings are for them, not for you.

We'll talk more about 1:1s in Chapter 7, where we'll walk through the GR8 1:1s Framework that further supports your shift from Chief Doer and Expert Problem-Solver to Coach. For now, just know that while 1:1s remain an essential connection point between you and each team member, an Ultra Leader knows how to get the most out of these conversations by rethinking their frequency and following the GR8 1:1s Framework.

KEEP LEARNING

If you want to read more about the ABCs, Team Road-maps, or TAPs, either pick up *The Next Normal* or head to *UltraLeadership.com* and *GregGiuliano.com* for downloadable templates and other resources.

A-B-C + 1-2-3 = POSITIVE TRANSFORMATION

Everything produces what it's designed to produce—the system laid out in this chapter produces Great Coaches. The caveat is that you must commit to it and make the shift from Manager (the usual and ordinary way) to Coach (the Ultra Leadership way).

The payoff for your commitment? A team that regularly performs above and beyond. A team that produces work of merit and impact. For them to produce work of merit and impact, you need them to be engaged, to feel empowered to shape their work, and to be activated to achieve their best. When people and teams are engaged, empowered, and activated, they will often perform above and beyond what is expected of them.

Getting there depends on you and how you show up every day. An average Leader produces average results. An Ultra Leader produces positive change by pushing the limits of what they can do. This doesn't mean working eighty-hour weeks or asking your team to do the same. Instead, it means pushing beyond the traditional "hard skills" expected of a Leader and learning to develop your "soft skills" instead.

We all have certain hard—or vocational—skills. But vocational skills aren't what make great Leaders or Coaches great. In the world of basketball, for instance, Coaches like Tara VanDerveer, John Wooden, and Steve Kerr all have superb vocational skills. But it's their soft skills—or what thought leader Simon Sinek refers to as *human skills*—that make them great. These Coaches know how to use these human skills to connect in the moment, to meaningfully interact with other people, and to get the best out of their teams.

I saw this approach in action during a recent coaching conversation with a Leader about succession planning. When asked about his criteria for choosing a successor, he said that he was looking for a combination of business acumen, empathy, and curiosity, with empathy and curiosity being more important than business acumen. The people he was considering all had tremendous business acumen, but he wasn't looking for usual and ordinary in a successor. He was looking for an Ultra Leader (like he is).

To become an Ultra Leader (who is also a Great Coach), put a premium on your human skills. Use your human skills to leverage your business acumen to create the conditions that make it easy for people to engage, feel empowered to shape their work, and achieve their best. Then you'll be able to build teams that don't need a Manager—teams that want a Coach.

Transformation Comes through People

All real leadership is change leadership because real Leaders enable *positive* transformation. Ultra Leaders create positive transformation in their organizations, whether by changing a structure, a process, a strategy, the way the company goes to market, or any number of things.

All real leadership is change leadership because real Leaders enable positive transformation.

Unfortunately, most change initiatives fail because Leaders fail to consider that change always begins with and depends on people. Ultra Leaders, on the other hand, understand that change begins with their teams. They know it's not enough to announce a structural or procedural change through an impersonal email and be done with it. Instead, they follow up and support the people they depend on to execute these changes.

That doesn't mean they try to change others. As I learned the hard way, coercing a team member into a change they don't understand or don't agree with often leads that team member to disengage or quit. If they can't find their place in the new order, they'll look for the door. Instead, Ultra Leaders help others want to change themselves.

How do you get there? You must continually work to provide people with opportunities to change. Ask yourself, *How can I help the people on my team to willingly, enthusiastically, and repeatedly be part of continuous transformation?* Why is this important? Because macro-level change requires micro-level change.

That said, change doesn't have to be complicated. At the end of the day, leadership is not rocket science. We have people to lead, and our job as Leaders is to engage and empower them. To engage and empower them, follow the ABCs. Align them. Build their capacity as individuals and teams. Coordinate their actions so that your plates are spinning in the same direction at the same time. Use Team Roadmaps and TAPs to generate alignment, Build individual and collective capacity, and Coordinate action.

If you want to take it to the next level and become an Ultra Leader, make an intentional shift from Manager to Coach. The rest of this book is all about you deciding to coach for a change—and by doing so, engaging and empowering people and activating their desire to change themselves.

All Real Leadership Is Change Leadership

Making the shift to a change mindset isn't always easy. Humans tend to resist change. I saw this recently, working with a client as they were designing and announcing a significant reorganization. When the changes were announced, an executive on the leadership team said, "Okay, the change is done. Now let's get back to business." He saw change as an inconvenient disruption, and as such, he labeled it as "bad."

However, according to Zen philosophy, change is neither bad nor good. To illustrate this point, in 1960, the philosopher Alan Watts shared "The Story of the Chinese Farmer" to illustrate this point.

Once upon a time, there was a Chinese farmer whose horse ran away. That evening, all of his neighbors came around to commiserate. They said, "We are so sorry to hear your horse has run away. This is most unfortunate." The farmer said, "Maybe." The next day the horse came back bringing seven wild horses with it, and in the evening, everybody came back and said, "Oh, isn't that lucky. What a great turn of events. You now have eight horses!" The farmer again said, "Maybe."

The following day his son tried to break one of the horses, and while riding it, he was thrown and broke his leg. The neighbors then said, "Oh dear, that's too bad," and the farmer responded, "Maybe." The next day the conscription officers came around to conscript people into the army, and they rejected his son because he had a broken leg. Again all the neighbors came around and said, "Isn't that great!" Again, he said, "Maybe."

The whole process of nature is an integrated process of immense complexity, and it's really impossible to tell whether anything that happens in it is good or bad—because you never know what will be the consequence of the misfortune; or, you never know what will be the consequences of good fortune.[8]

---

8   Jade Panugan, "'The Story of the Chinese Farmer,' by Alan Watts," Craftdeology, accessed August 12, 2024, https://www.craftdeology.com/the-story-of-the-chinese-farmer-by-alan-watts/.

The point is, it is our perspective and our response to change that determines whether the change we are experiencing is "good" or "bad."

The executive's statement reminded me of this story—and how we often think of change in unhelpful ways. After quietly chuckling to myself, I reminded him and the whole team that *this* was the moment when the hard work began in earnest. An old way of thinking about change is to see it as a cycle of order-disorder-order. In actuality, change is a cycle of *order-disorder-reorder*.[9] When it comes to leading change, there are yard markers and milestones, but there is no end zone.

Again, while it's become cliché to say that change is constant, that doesn't make it any less true. We need to adopt a change mindset that acknowledges this reality. When the change takes the form of a particular initiative (a reorganization, a merger, or an acquisition), changing the structure or systems and processes is the easy part. Some think this is all that change entails. It's not. Changing structures, systems, and processes requires a change in people's mindsets—not an easy task. But to lead change successfully, we need to direct much more of our attention to the people side of the equation.

Adopting a change mindset moves us to see change as normative and ongoing. A change mindset enables us to see

9   Richard Rohr, *The Wisdom Pattern: Order, Disorder, Reorder* (Cincinnati: Franciscan Media, 2020).

that organizational change initiatives must address cultural issues and leadership and workforce development as well as structure and systems and processes. In fact, cultural issues, leadership, and individual development will make or break any change effort in any organization. When we develop a change mindset, we also develop a flexibility and willingness to adjust how we implement change as a result. That leads to an intentional and continuous curiosity about how people are engaging and performing in relation to change.

We can get better at change. Acknowledging the perpetual nature of change should motivate us to cultivate a skill set that strengthens our capacity for continuous change leadership. Effective change leaders exhibit the ability to think critically, feel deeply, and communicate with precision. The competencies stemming from these foundational skills include the following:

1. **Managing Complexity:** Unraveling confusion, strategic thinking, and rapid problem-solving is paramount. According to McKinsey, organizations with effective change management are 3.5 times more likely to outperform their peers.[10]

---

10 McKinsey & Company, "How the Implementation of Organizational Change Is Evolving," February 5, 2018, https://www.mckinsey.com/capabilities/implementation/our-insights/how-the-implementation-of-organizational-change-is-evolving.

2. Innovating: Fostering creativity and positive
   disruption is essential for navigating dynamic
   landscapes. A study by Boston Consulting Group
   found that 79 percent of executives ranked innovation
   as a top-three priority for their organizations.[11]

3. Communicating: Designing, convening, and hosting
   crucial conversations, including coaching and
   feedback conversations, are pivotal to guide change.
   Towers Watson research reveals that companies with
   highly effective communicators achieve 47 percent
   higher total returns to shareholders.[12]

4. Executing: Setting goals, directing operations, and
   achieving objectives are key to effective change
   leadership. A study by Prosci indicates that
   organizations with excellent change management are
   six times more likely to meet project objectives.[13]

11 Boston Consulting Group, "Nearly 80% of Companies Worldwide Rank
    Innovation as a Top-Three Priority for 2023," May 23, 2023, https://www
    .bcg.com/press/23may2023-companies-rank-innovation-as-top-three-
    priority-2023.
12 Robert Sher, "Never Leave Internal Communications to Chance in
    Midsized Companies," *Forbes*, July 17, 2014, https://www.forbes.com/sites/
    robertsher/2014/07/17/never-leave-internal-communications-to-chance-
    in-midsized-companies/.
13 Tim Creasey, "Change Management Myths," Prosci, December 11, 2023,
    https://www.prosci.com/blog/change-management-myths.

5. Transforming: Generating awareness and fostering growth in oneself and others is fundamental for sustained change. Studies in psychology and behavioral science emphasize the importance of self-awareness in promoting change. Daniel Goleman's work on emotional intelligence, for instance, highlights that self-awareness is crucial for personal development and effective interpersonal relationships.[14]

Getting back to business does not mean reverting to the old ways. It means getting ready for the next change. And the next. And the next. A change mindset and a solid change leadership skill and competency set will support us in leading change over the long haul. It's vital that we are working toward this goal because change is never done. Remember, there is no end zone.

Remember, there is no end zone.

So, are you ready to lead differently and try coaching for a change?

TRUST THE PLAYERS

Let's have Steve Kerr bring our discussion about leadership to a close. When asked what he's learned as an NBA coach, Kerr said this:

---

14 Daniel Goleman, *Emotional Intelligence: Why It Can Matter More Than IQ* (New York: Bantam Books, 1995).

ARE YOU READY TO LEAD?

This self-survey is an opportunity to reflect on your ability to engage your team and your readiness to lean into coaching. Think about each item on this list. Rate yourself on a scale of one to five, with one meaning this item is an aspiration for you and five meaning the item is true for you all the time.

1. I provide a vision and clear strategy for my team.
2. I provide a clearly defined work breakdown structure (RACI) for my team.
3. I model and expect personal accountability.
4. I do not micromanage my team members.
5. I value my team members intrinsically and not just for what they produce.
6. I focus on results and productivity.
7. I encourage and support the ongoing development of my team members.
8. I have the business acumen and technical skills to support my team's efforts.

I've learned to trust [the players]. They're going to be the ones that determine wins and losses. And so your job as a coach is really to guide them and to try to put them in the best position and to not have this idea in your head that you are responsible for the ultimate success. That may sound like a paradox, because as a coach, that's your job: to win. But you've got to go in with the humility to understand that it's other people who are doing the work right. And the other people who are making the plays and having to compete.

I think understanding that dynamic has given me an understanding as coach that I'm really collaborating with and especially my key players, like Draymond Green, Steph Curry, we collaborate every day. I will readily take an idea of theirs in the heat of battle during middle of a game. ... It's important for me to embrace that and also not just succumb to whatever they think, but to work with them to get to the right and best solution. It's a really delicate balance.[15]

This statement by Coach Kerr really captures the essence of the type of leadership we need in our organizations today. Coach Kerr engages people. He empowers his team and activates them to shape their work and achieve their best. In that way, Coach Steve Kerr is an Ultra Leader, always working to

---

15   McCarvel, "Coach Steve Kerr."

identify gaps in knowledge, skills, or experience to help everyone on the team perform
above and beyond expectations.

Your team doesn't work for you. They work with you.

Your team doesn't work for you. They
work *with* you. Your role as team leader is
to collaborate with them to shape their work, guide them,
empower them, and activate them so they can win. You've
built a team that needs you to shift from Manager, Chief Doer,
and Expert Problem-Solver to Coach. That shift begins here.

EMBRACING A COACHING MINDSET

"COACHING TAKES FOREVER. IT'S JUST EASIER to tell my team what to do."

"Coaches aren't really Leaders."

"If I'm only coaching, I'm not creating value."

"Leaders should be in the trenches."

"My team needs me to solve problems for them."

These are some of the most common misconceptions about coaching I hear. Of course, they're not true. Not even a little bit.

Most Leaders are convinced of their need to be Chief Doer and Expert Problem-Solver for their team. Even after all these years, I still fight this urge too. We reach leadership positions because we're excellent at what we do and often know more about certain functions or capabilities than anyone else on the team. But, as author Marshall Goldsmith famously said, "What got you here won't get you there." The job of an effective Leader isn't to have all the answers or do all the work. It's to unlock the value in their team by helping people own their situation and find their own answers.

The job of an effective Leader isn't to have all the answers or do all the work. It's to unlock the value in their team by helping people own their situation and find their own answers.

And just to be clear, helping your team find their own answers is valuable. One small example: every Leader I've ever worked with who has tried coaching for a change has found that coaching saves them time. An effective coaching session can take as few as five minutes—far less time than an emergency all-nighter to pull your project back from the brink of failure.

You and your team work for a specific organization with a specific mission. The more people within that organization who are empowered to creatively and efficiently solve problems, the more your organization will succeed.

Research bears this out. In 2008, to understand what traits are common among the most effective leaders, Google began an ongoing study called Project Oxygen. They set out to discover what the most successful Managers do to engage people and lead high-performing teams. The research was extensive, and after a year's work, the Project Oxygen team identified eight behaviors that their best Managers had in common. In 2018, they amended their list to update two behaviors and add two more (three and six were updated; nine and ten were added in 2018).[16]

1. Be a good coach.
2. Empower; don't micromanage.
3. Create an inclusive team environment, showing concern for success and well-being.
4. Be productive and results-oriented.
5. Be a good communicator—listen and share information.
6. Support career development and discuss performance.
7. Have a clear vision/strategy for the team.
8. Have key technical skills to help advise the team.
9. Collaborate across the organization.
10. Be a strong decision-maker.

Notice a trend here? While the first behavior explicitly advocates for coaching, many of the rest—if not all the rest—describe the behaviors of a Great Coach. As Google learned through their Project Oxygen study, leaders who prioritize coaching consistently get the best results. It seems a Coach's

---

16 Scott Mautz, "Google Tried to Prove Managers Don't Matter. Instead, It Discovered 10 Traits of the Very Best Ones," *Inc.*, June 5, 2019, https://www.inc.com/scott-mautz/google-tried-to-prove-managers-dont-matter-instead-they-discovered-10-traits-of-very-best-ones.html.

success has less to do with their vocational skills in marketing or engineering than their ability to engage people and empower them to own their situation and find their own solutions.

The Project Oxygen results confirm my observation that Great Coaches share certain characteristics. The good news is you don't have to be born with those characteristics; anyone can become a Great Coach. And I don't just want you to try coaching for a change; I want you to be a Great Coach. To achieve this, however, you will have to take a leap of faith. Like a trapeze artist high above the crowd, you'll have to let go and fly to grab the other bar. Don't worry. This book will help you create your own net as you take the leap to being a Great Coach.

COACHING MEANS LETTING GO

Years ago, when I first stepped into a leadership role, I was convinced that my job as a Leader was to play the role of the Chief Doer and Expert Problem-Solver. So, I designed my team in a way where I was doing other people's work, because I liked doing that work and didn't want to let it go. I felt a need to control everything. As I would eventually learn, this approach led to a series of problems:

- By the time I'd "delegate," it was too late. I wasn't giving my team enough time to execute well, which frustrated and disempowered them. I was engaging their hands, but not their heads and hearts.

- I had created an unnecessary bottleneck. Worse, I chained the team's entire success to my own health and well-being. If something happened to me, all work would grind to a halt. I became a risk.

- I was making every project about me, rather than about my team. All our work was essentially just a stage for me to show my bosses what I could do in hopes of earning a few "attaboys."

As I got older and wiser, I realized that leading a team was not about me. But at the time, I was getting in everyone's way. I had yet to learn that Leaders serve the team; it isn't the other way around. I also had yet to learn that every system produces what it's designed to produce. If I'd understood that, I wouldn't have designed an environment that produced disengaged and disempowered team members. As a result, I was only getting a fraction of their talent.

Now ask yourself: Do you see a little bit of yourself in my story? Are you, like I was, too focused on controlling the process rather than creating the conditions for successful outcomes?

If you've set up the game so that it's a convoluted, mysterious puzzle that only you can solve, then you're not a Coach.

You're a problem. You're the one slowing everything down and creating an unnecessary risk for your organization.

Making the shift to start coaching for a change requires changing some beliefs you may have.

- Shift 1: Your team is not a machine. So, it's not your job to keep it running as precisely as a watch. Your team is a group of living, breathing people. How do you help them work together well? How do you help each individual to shape their work and achieve their best?

- Shift 2: Your team works *with* you, not for you. Yes, you have a particular role in that you set the mission and are likely the final decision-maker on some things. However, your primary role is to create the conditions for the team to succeed (and then get out of their way).

- Shift 3: You are not on the team you lead. Unless you're the CEO, you are on somebody else's team, with your own deliverables as a member of that team. Your team owns its work. Again, your job as a Leader is to take care of your team so that they can do their work.

Shifting your beliefs about teams and your role as Leader is the first step to becoming a Great Coach. Of course, the work doesn't stop there.

THE MINDSET OF A GREAT COACH

The starting point for great coaching is your mindset. Your mindset is your belief about something that determines how you act. In her book *Mindset: The New Psychology of Success*, researcher and author Carol Dweck describes how people operate on a spectrum, moving from a fixed to a growth mindset. The fact that you're reading this book may suggest you tend toward a growth mindset, motivating you to seek to learn and become a Great Coach to your people.

In the following discussion, we're going to explore the coaching mindset, the beliefs that will lead you to kick the Chief Doer and Expert Problem-Solver habit and try coaching for a change.

Coach the Person, Not the Problem

This is probably the hardest shift for Leaders to make when they want to shift from Manager to Coach. Coaches do not solve their team members' problems for them. Instead, they empower, ask questions, and draw the answers out. Remember, your job as a Coach is to support the development of the people on your team and enable positive transformation.

When you coach the problem instead of the person, three terrible things happen:

- You disempower. You send an implicit message that the person or the team can't own their situation or solve their problem. When you coach the problem, not the person, you're saying, "I don't trust you can do this."

- **You create dependency.** If you solve the problems all the time, even when "coaching," you're creating a culture of dependency. People will wait for you to tell them what to do. You may call it coaching, but you're just dressing up your expert problem-solving in new clothes.

- **You cause disengagement.** Whenever you say something along the lines of "Here's what you need to do," you're essentially telling your team to turn off their minds and blindly follow your commands.

That last point is worth underlining. As it turns out, disengagement is very expensive. Gallup's 2024 *State of the Global Workforce* found that, in 2023, only 23 percent of people reported feeling engaged at work. Because disengaged people are also less productive, this endemic lack of engagement was costing organizations $8.9 trillion *per year* globally.[17] Yikes.

Knowing that, repeat after me: you are not Lieutenant Columbo. Unlike the 1970s TV detective made famous by

---

17 Gallup, *State of the Global Workplace*, 2024, https://www.gallup.com/workplace/349484/state-of-the-global-workplace.aspx.

Peter Falk, your task is not to gather enough clues to solve the crime—or, in this case, enough information from a person to solve their problem. Your impatience and addiction to problem-solving will only lead you down the wrong path. (Ask me how I know.)

Instead, coach the person so they can solve their own problems. This forces you to be present, to be observant, to be curious. That curiosity will short-circuit your inner Columbo.

More importantly, your curiosity will naturally draw out the knowledge and natural ability someone needs to reconnect with to figure out how to own and transform their situation, transform themselves, or transform your team or company.

By ceding the decision-making power to your team member, you demonstrate trust in their abilities. "I know that the answer is in your head somewhere," you might say, "so let's get it out." In so doing, you build their sense of confidence and self-efficacy.

That last point is crucial. Often, when your team member comes to you with a problem, they are already aware of a solution. They're just afraid to pursue that solution on their own. Why? Because like so many of us, they were raised in the world of command and control. By default, they'll be inclined to seek approval before acting autonomously.

This is why coaching the person and not the problem is so powerful and a critical mindset to develop. It flips the old script. Instead of feeding the command-and-control dynamic, you empower people to commit to their own ideas.

Make Positive Assumptions

When you decide to coach the person, you are making a positive assumption about that person. Coaches make the positive assumption that people are capable. They get up in the morning. They function. They achieve. Coaches assume that the person has the knowledge, skills, experience, will, attitude, and aptitude to succeed. If they aren't succeeding, it's not a fundamental flaw within them, but rather the result of some barrier in their way. Our job is to help them identify anything blocking their way, find the best path forward, and accelerate toward the best next step.

Again, this mindset takes you out of Chief Doer and Expert Problem-Solver mode. You're not looking for a solution. You're working with your team member to understand what the block is, whether it's external or internal. In this mindset, the question is not "What's wrong with them?" but instead "How do I engage, empower, and activate them?"

Look to Learn

Great Coaches practice intentional curiosity. Be open to learning from the person you're coaching. As you try to

Great Coaches practice intentional curiosity.

help them understand their situation, don't assume you already know the answers. Approach the conversation with what the Zen Buddhists call a *beginner's mindset*. The beginner's mind relates directly to the characteristics of being present and observant. The beginner's mind is open and curious. The Leader or Coach with a beginner's mind is always looking to learn.

Sometimes this can be tricky, especially if you've known the team member for a while. Remember that just because you have prior knowledge of how a person thinks or behaves doesn't mean you know what they need or why they're stuck. The goal of every coaching conversation is to learn who the person is and what their situation is in that moment.

Staying open to solutions, change, and connection requires real listening. Most Leaders don't listen nearly enough, particularly if they're distracted. Just as you must be present to win the raffle, you must be present to lead and to listen. Don't just wait for your turn to speak. Be curious. Ask your team members what they need to be coached on, and then listen to their answers as you support them in looking for a solution.

Use Inquiry before Advocacy

Before telling someone what to do or what to know, ask questions.

Inquiry before advocacy fundamentally changes the nature of a conversation from declarative to collaborative. For instance, if I tell you that the sky is blue—that is, if I advocate for a position—you're now faced with a choice: agree or disagree. By making an affirmative statement or by telling you what to do, I immediately put you in a position where you must decide whether you agree.

Leading with advocacy rather than inquiry creates a few problems:

- **Unfair power dynamics.** Even if you disagree with me, because we're caught up in the Leader/team member power dynamic, you're still likely to agree with me—at least outwardly. I am the boss, after all, and I have just communicated that I have a solution and that any further exploration is unnecessary.

- **Trust issues.** I've once again found a way to communicate that I don't trust you to solve your own problems.

- **Disempowerment.** If you agree with the solution I just advocated for, you might still feel empowered. But if you disagree, you've begun to disengage because I have limited the scope of the conversation and taken away your agency.

A football Coach I know once told me he preferred the running game over the passing game because, as he said, "When you pass the ball, only one of three things can happen, and two of them are bad." (For those of you who aren't football fans, the pass could be incomplete, or worse, intercepted by the opposing team.) In some ways, advocacy is like passing the ball. As soon as you release the ball, you've committed yourself to a single action, with a two-thirds chance of negative consequences.

Inquiry, on the other hand, is more like a running game. You place the ball in your team members' hands, entrusting them to find a way forward, perhaps allowing them to discover a better solution that you never would have considered. Rather than putting your team in a position to vote on anything, you're just asking a question—and in so doing, drawing out the good ideas they likely already have.

When I was clinging to the mindset of Chief Doer and Expert Problem-Solver, I assumed that my people had an empty bucket that only I could fill. Great Coaches, however, neither fill the bucket nor hand someone a full bucket. Instead, they hand their team members an empty bucket— that is, the parameters for success—and ask, "What would you fill this with?"

Of all the coaching mindsets, I've found this to be one of the hardest for Leaders to adopt. After all, advocacy is a powerful drug. It's fast and easy, and it often leads to positive results in the short term.

As high-ranking Leaders, those results feel important to us. Accustomed to the command-and-control environment, we often make the mistake of thinking that our value rests exclusively with our vocational expertise, our knowledge, and our ability to tell people what to do. Following this logic, we believe that if we don't contribute or advocate, we are not demonstrating the expertise that justifies our position.

Again, that's simply not true. Increasingly, modern organizations seek Leaders who embody a coaching mindset, not an advocate-and-act mindset. Skipping over the inquiry part and inserting your own answers might fulfill your immediate needs, but in the long term, it is far more limiting for the organization and the individuals within it.

If you have a natural habit of advocating, here's your chance to step out of your comfort zone. Inquiry runs against the grain of that habit, which means adopting it will require intentionality and practice.

CHARACTERISTICS OF A GREAT COACH

Which came first, the chicken or the egg? Coaching begins with a certain mindset and utilizes a specific skill set, which we'll get to in the next chapter. When we develop a coaching mindset, we demonstrate certain characteristics. In *Ultra Leadership*, I talk about the six characteristics of a great Leader. It just so happens that these are also the six characteristics of a Great Coach. When we embody these characteristics, we cultivate the coaching mindset, and vice versa. When we cultivate a coaching mindset, we embody the characteristics of an Ultra Leader and a Great Coach.

1. Be Present

I had a client who wanted his team to know that he was "there for them." He wanted to be a Great Coach to his team. I explained that becoming a Great Coach starts with being present with people. "Oh, I'm totally present with people," he said.

"Are you sure?" I said before asking him if I could give him some feedback. "Over the past thirty minutes of our conversation, you have looked at your phone twelve times. How might I interpret that?"

He thought about it for a minute and replied, "Every time I looked at my phone, you probably thought that someone or something was more important to me." I didn't have to say anything.

I told him I shared his tendency, which was why I left my phone with my bag on the other side of his office before we sat down. I know I'm addicted to looking at my phone, and I know that I will feel compelled to check it if it's nearby, no matter who is seated at the table across from me. My simple way to break this habit is by distancing myself from the distracting object.

Being present means engaging others in a here-and-now experience you both share. Most of us aspire to this ideal, but practicing it is often challenging.

> Being present means engaging others in a here-and-now experience you both share.

It's not hard to see why. As a Leader, you work in a fast-paced and complex environment, where success is often measured in quarterly reports and bottom lines. Your attention is being pulled in many directions by external events and by your own emotions. You may be rethinking a meeting or conversation from earlier in the day, yesterday, or last week. You may be worried about something coming up tomorrow or next week. How can you be in the present moment with all that going on in your head? (To be clear, "be present" isn't code for "slow down." Being present actually helps you go faster and use your time more effectively.)

To be a Great Coach, you'll need to cultivate a way to keep yourself in the here and now. Some call this mindfulness.

So, what is mindfulness? The American Psychological Association defines mindfulness as "a moment-to-moment awareness of one's experience without judgment."[18] And research shows that practicing mindfulness can have significant benefits for Coaches, teams, and organizations. In an interview with the *Knowledge at Wharton* podcast, Dr. Lindsey Cameron discussed some of the personal benefits of mindfulness she and her researchers had found:

> First, from the higher-level picture, we did find that mindfulness made people more helpful at work. Then in terms of mechanisms, we found that perspective-taking—being able to look at someone else's perspective—was one of the reasons that mindfulness helped people become more effective. Empathy—the ability to feel what other people are feeling—also made people more helpful at work.[19]

18 Daphne M. Davis and Jeffrey A. Hayes, "What Are the Benefits of Mindfulness?," *Monitor on Psychology* 43, no. 7 (2012): 64.
19 Knowledge at Wharton Staff, host, *Knowledge at Wharton*, podcast, "Mindfulness at Work: A Little Bit Goes a Long Way," September 30, 2019,

When we are mindful, we have a greater capacity for careful thinking and strategic decision-making. This in turn leads to better results for the teams we lead. But the benefits don't stop there:

- In an article for *Business Horizons*, Hema Krishnan writes, "Leaders' commitment to mindfulness can have a positive impact on teams, which in turn can translate into collective mindfulness for the organization."[20]

- In the paper, Krishnan also cites research from Roche, Haar, and Luthans, stating, "Top managers can reap huge psychological and physiological benefits from consistent practice."[21]

- In her book *Real Happiness at Work*, Sharon Salzberg posits that mindfulness strengthens servant leadership attributes like balance, compassion, resilience, patience, concentration, and empathy.[22]

https://knowledge.wharton.upenn.edu/podcast/knowledge-at-wharton-podcast/mindfulness-at-work/.

20 Hema A. Krishnan, "Mindfulness as a Strategy for Sustainable Competitive Advantage," *Business Horizons* 64, no. 50 (2021): 697–709, https://doi.org/10.1016/j.bushor.2021.02.023.

21 M. Roche, J.M. Haar, and F. Luthans, "The role of mindfulness and psychological capital on the well-being of leaders," *Journal of Occupational Health Psychology* 19, no. 4 (2014): 476–489, https://doi.org/10.1037/a0037183.

22 Sharon Salzberg, *Real Happiness at Work* (New York: Workman Publishing, 2014).

- Finally, Erik Dane's and Bradley Brummel's research indicates that mindfulness contributes to bottom-line performance, as measured by traditional financial metrics, such as revenues and profits, as well as reduced employee turnover and reduced healthcare costs.[23]

In other words, mindfulness matters. By taking just a few moments a day to recenter yourself, you will improve your ability to get things done.

That said, be careful. Being present doesn't start when you sit down for a meeting. It's a state of being—and *not* our default setting. We seek distraction. Our memories and emotions pull us out of the present and into the past and future. Being present requires both practice and intentionality. When I recognize I'm not being present, I have to stop and find my way back. Here's a practice that works for me:

- Find a quiet place. (Close your door. Silence your phone.)
- Set a timer for two minutes. (I like the Samsara app.)
- Sit comfortably in your chair with both feet on the floor.

---

23 Erik Dane and Bradley J. Brummel, "Examining workplace mindfulness and its relations to job performance and turnover intention," *Human Relations* 67, no. 1 (2013): 105–128, https://doi.org/10.1177/0018726713487753.

- Focus on your breathing. Don't judge it. You're just breathing.
- Acknowledge whatever comes into your mind, then let it go and refocus on your breathing.

Commit to practicing this daily for eight weeks. When you're ready, increase your time from two to five minutes. Eventually, you'll notice that urge to glance at your phone or tune out during a meeting has all but disappeared. If it helps, keep a sticky note with the word "Breathe" on it in front of you.

Great Coaches are intentional about being present to themselves and to others. Larry Senn, founder of Senn Delaney and author of *The Mood Elevator*, says that leading well comes down to these three words: Be. Here. Now. That means being present. When we are present, we become empathetic, and empathy leads to curiosity and concern.

2. Be Observant

Another Leader I worked with asked me to sit in on a team meeting to observe him. During the meeting, I observed he wasn't really engaged until he would grow impatient and say something like "Here's what you need to do." He did that more than once with more than one team member. He demonstrated little curiosity. I thought, *If this is how he acts when I'm watching, what's it like when he's not on his best behavior?*

When he asked me how the meeting went, I shared my feedback with him. I asked him, "Can you tell me how many

questions you asked during the meeting today?" He stared
back blankly. "I'll give you a hint," I continued. "You'll only
need part of one hand to get to the total."

Curiosity is a sign that someone is observant and seeks
to understand. They're paying attention to what's going on
around them, and they're curious about what's occurring in
the field of their experience. We must be observant and con-
cerned about what is occurring in the field of our experience.
Being observant means assessing our current situation fully,
enabling careful thinking before we jump
into action.

**Great Leaders
and Coaches
are curious.**

Great Leaders and Coaches are curious.
They take the time to be observant, as demonstrated by an inclination to listen, inquire, synthesize, and
guide rather than immediately act.

3. Be Creative

Curiosity and creativity go hand in hand. When you're present
and observant, you become more creative. The more curious
you are as a Coach, the more creative you can be, allowing
you to sit in possibility longer. With this additional time
and space, you and the person you are coaching can identify issues and draw distinctions that lead to more optimal
solutions, rather than just the obvious ones. Curiosity drives
individuals to explore new ideas, ask questions, and consider
possibilities beyond the obvious. A study by Kashdan and
Silvia (2009) found that curiosity is associated with greater

cognitive flexibility and creativity.[24] This cognitive flexibility allows you to consider a wider range of options and possible solutions, exploring the opportunities in each one.

Leadership and coaching enable positive transformation—and transformation is a creative act. Leadership and coaching that enable positive transformation are inherently creative acts because they involve envisioning new futures and possibilities. A 2014 study published in *Journal of Management* emphasizes that creativity and innovation are central to transformational leadership.[25] When you embrace creativity, you are better equipped to guide those you are coaching through transformative processes, helping them to identify and implement innovative solutions.

Great Coaches invite and facilitate creativity. They strive to evoke the optimal solution in service of enabling positive transformation.

4. Be Innovative

Often, when we're not being as present or observant as we could be, we're not being very creative. When that happens,

24 Todd B. Kashdan and Paul J. Silvia, "Curiosity and Interest: The Benefits of Thriving on Novelty and Challenge," in *Oxford Handbook of Positive Psychology*, eds. Shane J. Lopez and C.R. Snyder (Oxford: Oxford University Press, 2009): 367–374.

25 Neil Anderson, Kristina Potočnik, and Jing Zhou, "Innovation and Creativity in Organizations: A State-of-the-Science Review, Prospective Commentary, and Guiding Framework," *Journal of Management* 40, no. 5 (2014): 1297–1333, https://doi.org/10.1177/0149206314527128.

we may drop an old solution into a new situation. What did we do last time? Let's do that again. Sometimes that works. Many times, it doesn't. In either case, the solution isn't innovative. It's just maintaining the status quo—doing the same thing we did yesterday to fix a new situation today.

With mundane activities, that repetition can work fine. I don't need to be innovative when I'm tying my shoes; I have a solution that works. But if I'm trying to figure out a new way to go to market, engage customers, or create value, innovation becomes increasingly important. Positive transformations for the organization, team, or individual often require an openness to innovate, to try something new that may not always be obvious at first glance.

The concept of *divergent thinking*, which involves generating multiple possibilities or solutions to a problem, is foundational to creativity and innovation. Research by Joy Paul Guilford on creativity emphasizes that the ability to generate multiple solutions is a key aspect of creative problem-solving.[26] Coaches who encourage clients to entertain various options engage in a process that fosters creativity and innovation.

Great Coaches help people entertain multiple options, allowing possible paths forward to emerge and multiply. At least one of them will likely be innovative—but only when we are present and observant enough to create space for

---

26 J.P. Guilford, *The Nature of Human Intelligence* (New York: McGraw-Hill, 1967).

intentional curiosity to invite creative thinking that produces innovation.

5. Be Strategic

Being strategic represents a shift in focus. The first four characteristics of a Great Coach are focused on expansive thinking
so that you and your team can take in as much information
as possible and generate a broad range of solutions. But at
this point, a Coach will say, "We've got all these great ideas
on the table. Some of them are really strong, but within this
context, we need to make a choice that's most effective for
our goals." A strategy is a choice.

Jeanne Liedtka is a strategist and professor at the University of Virginia's Darden Graduate School of Business. Her
research on strategic thinking emphasizes that this process
involves both rational analysis and creative insight. When you
guide someone through strategic thinking, you help them
weigh options and consider the underlying assumptions and
implications of each choice, leading to more informed and
aligned decisions.[27]

Research by Cox, Bachkirova, and Clutterbuck (2014)
highlights that coaching enhances a person's ability to
think critically and reflectively.[28] Great Coaches help people

---

27 Jeanne M. Liedtka, "Linking strategic thinking with strategic planning,"
    Strategy & Leadership 26, no. 4 (1998): 30–35, https://www.proquest.com/
    docview/194364332?sourcetype=Scholarly%20Journals.
28 Elaine Cox, Tatiana Bachkirova, and David Clutterbuck, eds., *The Complete*

choose by weighing all the options, considering the underlying assumptions and implications of each one, and making a decision that aligns with their highest intent.

6. Be Purposeful

Being purposeful means acting with intention. As my friend and former CEO Janet Widmann said during an interview for my book *Ultra Leadership,*

> We can go very fast. We pride ourselves on getting lots of stuff done in a short amount of time. It takes leadership to think carefully, to stop when necessary, and ask, "Where are we? What are we trying to create or achieve? What are the possibilities for next steps?" It takes leadership to make sure we're being productive and not just busy. Careful thinking ensures we are connected to our mission and our purpose for going so fast and trying to get so much done. It is leadership informed by careful thinking that ensures we're being intentional with how we're spending our time and energy.

The role of coaching in moving from idea to outcome is supported by research on goal-setting and action planning. Locke and Latham (2002) found that setting clear, purposeful goals is crucial for transforming ideas into tangible

Handbook of Coaching (New York: SAGE Publications, 2014).

outcomes.[29] Coaches help coachees focus their thoughts and actions on these goals, providing the structure and accountability needed to generate momentum and achieve results. When we connect with purpose, we shift from being busy to being productive. Great Coaches focus thought and action, generating momentum to move from idea to outcome.

RETHINK AND RESET TO RENEW

In order to reset how we show up as Leaders, we need to be ready to rethink things from time to time, as I wrote in *The Next Normal*. Our discussion of the coaching mindset and the characteristics of Ultra Leaders and Great Coaches provides an opportunity to rethink how we're showing up at present and reset as a Great Coach. Take some time to reflect on the following to engage in your own process of rethinking and resetting.

> Rethink: How present are you? Do you find yourself reliving past events or worrying about the future?
> How might you grow your capacity to "be here now"?
> Reset: What is one concrete step you could take today to be more present?

---

29 Edwin A. Locke and Gary P. Latham, "Building a practically useful theory of goal setting and task motivation: A 35-year odyssey," *American Psychologist* 57, no. 9 (2002): 705–717, https://doi.org/10.1037/0003-066X.57.9.705.

Rethink: How observant are you? Are you intentionally curious?

Reset: How might you remind yourself to ask more questions of yourself and others?

Rethink: How do you invite and facilitate creativity and innovation?

Reset: How might you design your conversations and meetings to unlock creativity and innovative thinking?

Rethink: How careful and strategic is your thinking? What criteria factor into your decision-making?

Reset: What one shift would ensure your thinking is more careful and strategic?

Rethink: Are you clear about how you intend to be and what you intend to do? How does your intention drive your decision-making about how you show up as a Leader to engage others?

Reset: How would you describe your leadership if you're leading "on purpose"?

Rethinking is the easy part. Resetting is harder. It takes intentionality. We become Great Coaches through practice. Practice is more about routines and rituals than will and discipline. Design your schedule to include space and time to practice. What new routines and rituals can support your desire to be a Great Coach to your team? Your dedication and consistency will bring about your renewal. You will show up in a new way, being more present and observant, creative and innovative, strategic and purposeful. That will shift your mindset about coaching. And that will require you to develop some skills that are of particular use as you make the shift from Manager to Coach. In the next chapter, we'll explore the specific coaching skills and behaviors that lead to better results—for both you and your team.

As you begin to incorporate the concepts in this chapter into how you lead, please remember two things. First, be kind to yourself. These concepts are easy to understand, but far more difficult to master. Second, be honest with yourself about your habits and be open to feedback from others who are on the receiving end of your leadership and coaching.

The best way to do this is to intentionally ask someone to help keep you on track. Coaches who seek coaching and feedback model accountability. I used to tell my patients that only healthy people go to therapy, for they know something isn't right. No one really needs coaching. Nothing's broken. But the most successful people in every profession seek out coaching to help them learn, grow, and get better. Coachability is another key characteristic of a Great Coach. We intentionally and repeatedly step into the cycle of order-disorder-reorder. We take our own medicine. We lead by example.

> Coachability is another key characteristic of a Great Coach. We intentionally and repeatedly step into the cycle of order-disorder-reorder.

**COACHING CHECKPOINT:
ASPIRATION OR TRUTH**

When you think about making the shift from Manager to Coach, some beliefs and behaviors may already be true for you, while some others may still be aspirational. To find out, once you've walked through this rethink/reset exercise, try the following self-assessment:

1. On a scale of never to all the time, how would you respond to "I love solving other people's problems" (like most of us)? What might you do to kick that habit?

2. On a scale of never to all the time, how would you respond to "I trust other people's intentions and their ability to contribute"? How might you remind yourself to assume positive intent and ability more consistently?

3. On a scale of "I'm done" to all the time, how would you respond to "Are you open to learning new things and changing your behavior?" How might you restart or accelerate your learning and development?

4. On a scale of never to all the time, how would you respond to "I ask questions to learn what others think before I state my opinion"? How might you remind yourself to ask more questions and give more space to others to share their thoughts?

3

DEVELOPING A COACHING SKILL SET

WHO WOULD YOU RATHER WORK FOR: Logan Roy from *Succession* or Ted Lasso from, well, *Ted Lasso*?

In case you haven't watched either of these shows, here's a brief breakdown of the characters.

Logan Roy, played to ruthless perfection by actor Brian Cox, is the billionaire head of a multimedia conglomerate, sort of like a fictional Rupert Murdoch. He's a throwback to the command-and-control era, a tyrant with a "do what I say or you're out" mentality.

Then there's Ted Lasso, played with unbridled glee by *Saturday Night Live* alum Jason Sudeikis. As we've noted, Ted knows nothing about soccer. Everyone around him has forgotten more about soccer than he knows—including his wunderkind kit man, Nate. Perhaps because he's out of his element or perhaps because it's just his way (I like to think it's the latter), Ted leads with empathy. He listens to others. He's curious. He gives feedback in a caring way, making you know he wants to help you improve. His style is collaborative, inviting, and empowering. For instance, when he sees what a brilliant strategist Nate is, he promotes him to an assistant coaching role on the team.

Logan Roy and Ted Lasso possess and leverage very different skill sets. Logan Roy is not a Coach. He's a dictator, an extreme example of the command-and-control authoritarian style of leadership. By contrast, Ted Lasso is the definition of a Coach—a clear model for the kinds of leadership and coaching skills promoted by Google's Project Oxygen research (see Chapter 2). If you watch Ted closely, he almost never tells anyone what to do. He empowers them to think differently about their situation, so they find their own solution.

Interestingly, despite the fact that the characters and narratives of these two shows couldn't be more different, *Succession* and *Ted Lasso* have been two of the most-watched, most-acclaimed shows of the early 2020s. Where the former exemplifies the old command-and-control model the world is moving away from, the latter offers a model for what the world could be moving toward.

That's what the focus of this chapter is: honing the skills and behaviors necessary to thrive as a Leader in the world that's emerging. Real leadership is not a command; it's an invitation. Could Ted have walked into his new role and tried to coerce his new team into complying? He could have tried—and it might have even worked at first—but that approach has a limited shelf life. Follow the command-and-control model like Logan Roy, and your team members will disengage, do just enough to get by, get caught up in politics, or leave.

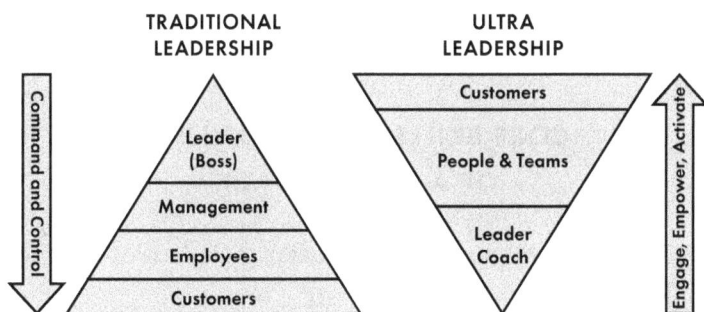

Why? Because, in a command-and-control organization, all effort is focused on appeasing the Leader rather than serving the team or the company's goals. Your team might have strong vocational skills, and they might run their verticals well, but they won't collaborate—and they certainly won't work horizontally across the organization. A leadership team that works well horizontally won't undermine others for their own gain. They think more about the entire enterprise. They make decisions keeping "we" instead of "me" in mind.

This is why Ted succeeds as a soccer Coach even when he knows so little about the sport. He creates the conditions for his team to engage, to feel empowered to shape their work, and to achieve their best. In reality, given how soccer is played, Ted has little other choice. Once the match starts, the Coach can send in a set play, but really, the leadership is on the pitch. The Coach prepares the team to work together so they'll be ready to make their own decisions on the field. In that way, leadership throughout the game shifts from player to player, depending upon where they are and what the situation calls for.

CORE SKILLS AND BEHAVIORS
OF A GREAT COACH

Perhaps that's the greatest byproduct of great Leader-Coaches: more Leaders.

Creating that culture of shared leadership, though, requires a much different skill set than the old command-and-control model. The skills of coaching are the "soft" or human skills we introduced in Chapter 1. As we get better at coaching, we become better humans. We demonstrate the characteristics of leadership and engage with empathy, warmth, and unconditional positive regard to enable transformation. Great Coaches are active listeners, adept at asking great questions, able to communicate directly and clearly deliver feedback, and exhibit real emotional intelligence. In this chapter, we'll explore these core skills and behaviors that will make you a Great Coach.

Active Listening

Active listening is a critical skill for coaching. The Greek Stoic philosopher Epictetus said, "We have two ears and one mouth so that we can listen twice as much as we speak." This ancient wisdom emphasizes that effective communication is not just about being able to express our own thoughts and ideas but also about attentively hearing and understanding others.

> We have two ears and one mouth so that we can listen twice as much as we speak.

The term "active listening" was coined by psychologists Carl Rogers and Richard Farson. As an existential-humanistic psychologist, Rogers believed that humans are responsible for and capable of their own growth. We facilitate that experience when we engage others with empathy, warmth, and unconditional positive regard or concern without judgment. Active listening is a way to express these principles. In fact, Rogers believed that the ultimate goal of active listening is to enable positive change. This is only one of many reasons I like Carl Rogers.

By listening more than we speak, we show respect, empathy, and openness, which are essential for building strong relationships and gaining deeper insights. In leadership, particularly, this approach fosters trust and collaboration, as it allows Leaders to truly understand the needs and perspectives of their team members. Ultimately, Epictetus reminds us that listening is a vital skill that enhances our ability to connect with and learn from others. Rogers and Farson remind us that it is through active listening that we enable another person's positive transformation.

All this begs the question: How do you know when someone *isn't* actively listening to you?

This isn't a scientific answer, but generally, you can just tell. The person isn't making eye contact. They're distracted. They may jump in and cut you off, not allowing you time to express your thoughts. Maybe they respond with a judgment or try to cut to the chase and tell you what to do.

It doesn't feel good when someone does any of these things, does it? But here's the thing: You do it too and so do I. So does everyone...at least sometimes. Think about it. When you're engaged in a conversation, how often do you do the following?

- Look at your phone?
- Wait for opportunities to make your own point?
- Immediately vote in your head when you agree or disagree with the person?
- Jump on opportunities to present yourself as the Expert Problem-Solver?
- Listen for reasons to validate your point of view?
- Look for a chance to escape the conversation?

If you do any of these things, and we all do, you may be hearing, but you're not actively listening. Sure, you might be hearing the words the person is saying, but you're not engaged in the substance of what they're saying in a meaningful way.

This brings us to the inverse question: How do you know someone *is* actively listening to you?

When someone is actively listening, you can see that they're directly focused on you. Their body language lets you know. The expression on their face conveys their empathy and warmth. They give you space and time to get out your thoughts. They don't jump to judgment. They may invite you to share more details to provide a fuller picture of your situation. And they can reflect back and summarize what you've told them. An old therapist's technique is to say, "What I hear you saying is..." and then ask the person, "Did I get that right?"

In almost any scenario, active listening will lead to greater understanding and better outcomes for nearly everyone involved. As actor, director, and author Alan Alda put it,

> The difference between listening and pretending to listen, I discovered, is enormous. One is fluid, the other is rigid. One is alive, the other is stuffed. Eventually, I found a radical way of thinking about listening. Real listening is a willingness to let the other person change you. When I'm willing to let them change me, something happens between us that's more interesting than a pair of dueling monologues.[30]

---

30 Alan Alda, *Never Have Your Dog Stuffed: And Other Things I've Learned* (New York: Random House, 2005).

When we are really listening, we are open to being moved by the other person and learning something from what they're saying. We listen for what's actually going on with the person we're coaching, rather than trying to confirm our assumption about what they need. Do they have a clear understanding of what the company is trying to accomplish and their responsibility to that goal? Do they have the resources they need? What's behind the behaviors or feelings they're describing?

To get those answers, you'll have to practice active listening. Like any skill, active listening takes time to master. Active listening is almost never our default setting. It takes intention and practice. This is a muscle we all must exercise regularly.

All of the practice pays off, though, because active listening is a way of setting up your team members for success. It gives you the opportunity to be present and observant, to ask meaningful questions, and to learn from the person or people in front of you. This in turn will give your own questions and responses more credibility.

The Three Levels of Listening

For any Coach, listening represents an essential skill. The Co-Active Training Institute, one of the preeminent coaching training organizations in the country, offers a program that teaches the three levels of listening.[31] The location of

---

31 Co-Active Training Institute, "The Three Levels of Listening," November 30, 2022, https://coactive.com/resources/blogs/levels-of-listening.

your attention distinguishes one level from another. I find this to be an excellent model for understanding and practicing active listening. Let's take a look!

Level 1: Internal

What happens in your head as you're listening? Often, you're caught up in your own role as a listener. For example, you might feel preoccupied by figuring out your response to what you're hearing, you might be thinking about the ways in which you can implement the other person's ideas, or you might get distracted by a cute person passing by.

Regardless of the details, at this level, you are only partially present to the other person's words. While they talk, you are simultaneously considering what to say in response or how to develop the ideas they are communicating to you. You are focused more on yourself as a listener than you are on the speaker in front of you.

Level 2: Focused

In the second level of listening, you truly listen to the speaker. The focus shifts from your internal experience to the other person. You dial in on the speaker's words, give them your complete attention, and successfully block out distractions. You're not thinking about the past or the future, and you are not busy in your mind formulating a response to what you've heard. You simply focus on the speaker's words, trying to understand what they're saying.

Level 3: Global

The third level of listening considers the listener and speaker as a team, involving wholehearted, fully empathetic attention. As a listener, you do not simply process the other person's words. You also pay attention to their body language, nuances in tone, inflections of speech, and affectations. Where does the speaker pause and hesitate? Where do they seem to have the most intensity or deepest level of articulation? You attempt to tune in to the speaker's inner experience, interpreting more than just the language you hear.

At this level, you are really trying to understand who the speaker is in the conversation and what they've brought with them that might not be immediately apparent in their words. Words devoid of this context do not have their full meaning. To reach this context, the listener needs to develop interpretive empathy.

Here's the long and short of interpretive empathy. As a listener, if I'm not willing to be changed by you, I'm not really listening to you. The listener reaches the third level of listening by being fully present and observant, attempting to take on the speaker's perspective in order to more deeply understand the motivations behind the information. The listener focuses on who the speaker is and how they are speaking, in addition to what they are saying. This depth of openness accepts the possibility of being changed by the speaker's words through profound engagement.

In some ways, the path to this third level of listening is similar to a meditative practice. In meditation, you try to clear your mind, but thoughts will inevitably intrude. You learn to acknowledge those intrusions and then let them fall away, always returning to the breath. In this analogy, the breath could be the words and presence of the person speaking. Notice when you are distracted, and then simply return to the person who is speaking to you.

Exercise: Listen Up

The "Listen Up" exercise is a mainstay of our Be a GR8 Coach Program. In this exercise, your goal is to grow your capacity to demonstrate warmth, empathize, and listen without judgment.

If you want to try this exercise, you're going to need a partner. Here's how you do it:

1. For five minutes, have your partner talk about what they hope people say about what it's like to work with them.
2. During this time, you're only allowed to ask questions for clarification.
3. Pause to reflect on what that experience was like, and then switch roles.
4. At the end of the exercise, discuss the following questions:
   - What was that experience like? (Both)
   - Did you feel listened to? (Speaker)

- How could you tell? (Speaker)
- What did you hear that was "under the facts"? (Listener)
- What was easy or difficult about maintaining focus and actively listening? (Listener)
- How could listening in this way help you more completely engage and develop your team? (Both)

Inquiry: Asking Strong Questions

The ability to ask strong questions is vital to coaching. Using inquiry before advocacy is an element of the coaching mindset. When I facilitate team conversations, I sometimes break the team into small groups to open the discussion and get full participation. If the Team Leader wants to participate, I give an explicit instruction: "If you're going to sit in on a conversation, you can only ask questions. We want to know what the team thinks, not align them to what you think." Asking strong questions is a skill we never stop developing.

Some questions lead to more productive conversations than others. Strong questions generate dialogue. They start with *when, where, what, why, who,* or *how.* They are open-ended and can't be answered with a simple "yes" or "no."

A terrific Coach I worked with early in my career told me to avoid what he called *queggestions*: suggestions disguised as questions. Queggestions sound like "Have you tried...?" or "What if you...?" Inquiry helps you remember you're coaching the person, not the problem. It keeps you learning. Learn more and encourage your team members to consider what's in their power to change. Ultimately, the answers to those questions drive business results.

Great Coaches ask strong questions—and then, because they practice active listening, they're attentive to the responses. Used in tandem, active listening and inquiry provide the foundation for every coaching conversation. Listen well, and then ask questions that demonstrate you've heard the other person well and accurately. Through your inquiry, you unlock their ability to rethink, reset, and renew. You cultivate an intellectual independence as they learn they can creatively face whatever comes their way.

Through your inquiry, you help another person become more present and observant, creative and innovative, and strategic and purposeful. By actively listening and asking strong questions, you engage and empower people, activating them to achieve their best.

Direct Communication (a.k.a. Giving Feedback)

Tell me if this situation sounds familiar: you need to have a hard conversation with one of your team members about their performance, but you've been avoiding it because you're not sure how to approach it.

This is the situation a good 75 to 80 percent of the Leaders I work with describe to me during our Be a GR8 Coach workshops. They want to be better at direct communication and offering feedback, even if they're often terrified to follow through.

I watched this happen way back when I was a baby Coach running leadership development workshops and teaching people about giving better feedback. We taught participants how to give feedback. It quickly became clear that even though they knew constructive feedback was a good idea, and even though we'd given them tools to help those conversations go better, these aspiring Leader-Coaches were still avoiding the hard conversations. Why? The quick answer most gave was they didn't want to hurt someone's feelings. The more honest answer is that they were uncomfortable delivering difficult information. Either way, they weren't practicing what they learned.

Direct conversations are hard—and very few of us like being uncomfortable. To become a Great Coach, however, perhaps nothing is more important than tackling that discomfort head-on. Letting time pass doesn't fix anything, but it can make things worse. Problems compound if given time— so don't give them any time.

When you see a questionable behavior over time, or see work products that don't meet expectations, talk about it. From time to time, you will have to give someone feedback about their performance. Author and thought leader Adam Grant says there are three keys to doing this:

1. Be a Coach, not a critic. Aim to help, not attack.
2. Don't assert opinion as fact. You're sharing your subjective reaction, not the objective truth.

3. Be honest, not brutal. Be direct in what you say, but kind in how you say it.[32]

Effective feedback isn't about sharing your opinion of what's good or bad; it's about drawing a direct line between specific behaviors and specific outcomes. I've found that feedback happens best in the context of a coaching conversation. When I understand your intention, I can provide feedback as to how your actions are helping you or hindering you in achieving what you intend. That's better than cold-calling you and dropping feedback on you. If I do that, I'm probably giving you feedback to make me feel better, not help you get better.

There are real, tangible benefits to developing this skill. Constructive feedback is vital for personal and professional growth. According to Gallup, employees who receive regular feedback are 3.6 times more likely to be engaged at work than those who do not.[33] So how do we get better at giving feedback?

According to Gallup, employees who receive regular feedback are 3.6 times more likely to be engaged at work than those who do not.

---

32 Adam Grant (@AdamMGrant), "How to give feedback without being a jerk...," X, November 17, 2023, https://twitter.com/AdamMGrant/status/172557431065435786.

33 Jason Evanish, "Key Takeaways from the Gallup State of the American Workplace Study," *Lighthouse Blog*, 2024, https://getlighthouse.com/blog/gallup-state-of-the-american-workplace-study/.

In Giving, We Receive

When I realized our program participants were avoiding giving feedback, we changed the assignment.

While we used to assign giving feedback as field work back in the day, we now ask them to practice seeking out feedback. Feedback is a gift. (Yes, even negative feedback.) Great Coaches seek it out. Ask someone you trust and who sees you in action to give you feedback. Tell them what you are working to develop. Maybe it is asking more and better questions. Ask them how you're doing. Ask them for evidence. What have they observed? What's the impact? Then say, "Thank you." They just gave you a gift. When you ask for feedback and show appreciation for the information you receive, you model openness. Nine times out of ten, people will then ask you for feedback in return. And *there's* your chance to practice giving feedback! I know, I'm tricky sometimes.

Second, I encourage Leaders to practice giving positive feedback. No one gets enough positive feedback. When you see that someone on your team is doing things right (which should be happening quite often), share what you've observed to reinforce those behaviors. Feedback doesn't have to be about problems; it can also endorse and reinforce desirable behaviors.

When offering positive feedback, again, be specific. Don't just compliment. Endorse a behavior or practice that you'd like to see more of, one that you think has a positive impact on people and the business. Note specific behaviors, such as an excellent question someone asked in a meeting, a particularly helpful way of organizing a report, or an approach to client service that went above and beyond. What you highlight will become a behavior your whole team will want to replicate.

I encourage every Leader I coach to find at least one person, once a week, and give some positive feedback. Become known as the most appreciative Leader in your organization.

Exercise: Endorsements and Illuminations

For this "Endorsements and Illuminations" exercise, you can grab your training partner or someone you trust and ask for feedback. Or you can have a team meeting and begin building a culture of regular feedback.

In this conversation, you are asking your feedback partner for an endorsement and an illumination. An endorsement is a comment on something you do that has a positive impact on the other person, the team, or the business. An illumination is a comment about a behavior or practice of yours that you may be unaware of that detracts from your desired impact, that may diminish you or another person. It's like when someone tells you that you have spinach in your teeth. You didn't know. Once you do know, you can remove the spinach. We all need someone who cares enough about us to tell us when we have spinach in our teeth.

Here's what to do if you're asking your training partner:

1. Say, "I'd like some feedback."
2. Ask, "Can you tell me something I do that is really good and I should do more of?" Listen to their feedback.
3. Then ask, "What is something I do that I may or may not be aware of that hinders my ability to succeed?" Another way to phrase this question: "How am I getting in my own way?"
4. Whatever you hear in response, just say, "Thank you," because no matter what they say, they're giving you a gift. You now have greater awareness about yourself than you had before. As a result, you can do more of what's working and change what isn't.

If you decide to do this feedback exercise as a team-building activity, you may want to set it up by saying something like the following:

Trust is critical if we're going to be a high-performing team. I've learned that feedback is a gift that generates trust. When someone gives me feedback, it tells me that person cares about my development and my performance. So, I'd like us to have a party now, a feedback party.

We're going to pair up and offer one another feedback. We're going to share an endorsement and an illumination. An endorsement is something that you are doing that is terrific, is having a positive impact on another person, the team, or our business. An illumination is something that we may be doing that we are not aware of that may be hindering our ability to achieve what we set out to achieve. An illumination may be a way we get in our own way. It's like being told if we have spinach in our teeth. That's an illumination. Only people who care about us will tell us we have spinach in our teeth.

So, we'll pair up and ask for feedback. It won't take us a long time. Five minutes each way should do it. Then we'll talk about what it was like.

When time is up, ask everyone how it went. They don't need to share the feedback that they got. You want the team to have a conversation that reinforces the positive nature of giving and receiving feedback. Ask them if this is something you might make a team routine. Invite them to find a feedback partner on the team and do this regularly on their own.

The more you model asking for feedback, the more you begin to normalize the giving and receiving of feedback, which creates a culture of trust and mutual development. Once you have built this culture of feedback, you'll find that (a) it's not so hard to hear or provide, and (b) both you and your team are far more likely to act on that feedback, accelerate your development, and increase your effectiveness. (We'll go into how to give feedback to boost performance in Chapter 9.)

Emotional Intelligence

Earlier, I suggested that when it comes to leading to engage, empower, and activate people, human skills are more important than vocational skills. Emotional intelligence is one of the most important human skills. In fact, emotional intelligence may be more conducive to success than cognitive intelligence. It is vital to successful leadership and coaching.

Human skills are more important than vocational skills.

So what is it? To paraphrase Daniel Goleman, a leading voice on emotional intelligence, emotional intelligence is the ability to regulate one's response to emotion, manage the emotional impact on decision-making, read the emotions of others, and act appropriately in relationships. According to Goleman, four inherent abilities collectively define emotional intelligence: self-awareness, self-management, social awareness, and relationship management.

Self-Awareness

Self-awareness is the foundation of emotional intelligence. Many of us believe we are self-aware when, in fact, we aren't. According to research by organizational psychologist Tasha Eurich, 95 percent of individuals believe they are self-aware, while in actuality only 12 to 15 percent are.[34] It is a lack of

---

34 Chad Gordon, "The Importance of Self-Awareness with Tasha Eurich," *Leaderchat*, February 1, 2019, https://leaderchat.org/2019/02/01/the-importance-of-self-awareness-with-tasha-eurich/.

self-awareness that is the root cause of most leadership failures. An emotionally intelligent Leader is aware of his own emotions and the impact of those emotions on his behavior. He is capable of assessing his emotional state, describing it, and making the connection between those emotions and his actions.

Self-Management

We cannot control our emotions. As we grow in emotional intelligence, we get better at managing how we respond to our emotions. That is what the second element of emotional intelligence is, the capacity for self-management. We grow the ability to lead ourselves and regulate our responses to emotion through self-dialogue. We learn to talk ourselves back to a state of calm. Self-management, the regulation of emotional response, is the capacity to contain our emotions, negative or positive, and remain calm in charged situations.

Self-management is characterized by transparency, adaptability, achievement, initiative, and optimism. The self-managing person is transparently living their values, adapts to challenging situations, pragmatically works to achieve goals, and is an optimistic self-starter. Self-management is what enables us to get started on, pay attention to, and finish work. Self-management helps us focus on a task or a series of tasks and sustain the required level of care over an extended period of time, even when the work is less than stimulating. Our capacity for self-management is what provides a sense of groundedness that enables us to self-impose a structure and a discipline to how we engage our work and other people in service of realizing our goals.

Social Awareness

Social awareness involves fostering an environment that supports healthy relationships within and between people, teams, and groups. The socially aware person is empathetic and able to tune in to and respond to the emotions of others. They are aware of the social and political realities of the groups and organization in which they operate.

Relationship Management

Our self-awareness, emotional self-management, and social awareness combine to support the fourth element of emotional intelligence: relationship management. Relationship management entails an ability to inspire, influence, and develop others. As Leaders, it enables us to engage, empower, and activate people to better foster teamwork, inspire cooperation, and facilitate strong collaboration.

In other words, it's not all about you, or me, as I learned when working to become a better and more effective therapist and then Coach. First, I became aware of my need to be the guy with the answers. Then, in order to behave differently, I had to identify the emotions that drove that behavior and manage my responses to those emotions. Making that shift enabled me to become more attuned to what was going on with someone else and to effectively engage them in the therapeutic, coaching, or personal relationship.

I tell this story to convey my strong belief that emotional intelligence is a skill that we can develop. Becoming more emotionally intelligent is a lifelong journey and takes regular practice.

Exercise: Emotional Intelligence—a Look in the Mirror

Here's an activity to start or restart your journey toward increasing self-awareness. How emotionally intelligent do you think you are today? A Leader I knew once told his team that the Leader's best friend is a mirror. It's good to hold it up every now and then and take an honest look.

In the following pages, you will find a self-survey of emotional intelligence. The survey is based upon Daniel Goleman's model of emotional intelligence. There are four categories in the survey: Self-Awareness, Self-Management, Social Awareness, and Relationship Management.

Scoring is on a scale of one (1) to three (3). Determine your score for a category by dividing the total score by the number of capabilities listed in that category. For example, in the Self-Awareness category, there are twelve items listed. Divide your total by twelve to get your score for Self-Awareness.

Each number in the scale represents the following descriptors of your level of ability regarding an element of emotional intelligence:

- This is an area I need to improve. This is a clear area of development.
- I am proficient at this.
- I am masterful. I could teach this. I practice this consistently.

At the conclusion of the survey, there will be some questions to spark further reflection and action planning, to grow your emotional intelligence in the areas where you identify development opportunities.

Self-Awareness

I recognize how my emotions affect me and impact my job performance.	I	2	3
I know what is most important to me and use my core values to apply perspective in complex situations.	I	2	3
I can easily talk about my feelings with candor and authenticity.	I	2	3
I can easily convey my highest purpose in life to others.	I	2	3
I am fully aware of my strengths and weaknesses.	I	2	3
I am able to laugh at myself.	I	2	3
I am open to feedback and seek it out on a regular basis.	I	2	3
I have a strong desire to learn.	I	2	3
I play to my strengths.	I	2	3

I welcome challenges.   1   2   3

I feel a strong sense of self-confidence.   1   2   3

I have a strong presence.   1   2   3

Add circled items to calculate your total score.
Divide your total by the number of items (12) to get your
Self Awareness score.

Self-Management

I have a strong capacity for managing negative
emotions and counterproductive impulses.   1   2   3

I can calm myself fairly quickly.   1   2   3

I remain clearheaded in stressful situations.   1   2   3

I handle confrontations easily and with a calm
directness.   1   2   3

I live my values.   1   2   3

I easily share my feelings, beliefs, and motivations.   1   2   3

I freely admit my mistakes and shortcomings.   1   2   3

I address unethical behavior when I see it.   1   2   3

I can juggle multiple demands without losing focus or
energy.   1   2   3

I am comfortable with uncertainty.   1   2   3

I easily adapt to new challenges and adjust my thinking
and behavior in the face of change.   1   2   3

I have high personal standards that drive me to continuously improve.	I	2	3
I regularly set personal and professional goals for myself and work to achieve them.	I	2	3
I am in control of my destiny.	I	2	3
I create opportunities rather than wait for them to arrive.	I	2	3
I do not hesitate to cut through red tape or bend the rules to achieve success.	I	2	3
I roll with the punches.	I	2	3
I see opportunities in setbacks.	I	2	3
I expect the best of people.	I	2	3
I see the glass as "half full."	I	2	3

Add circled items to calculate your total score.
Divide your total by the number of items (20) to get your
Self-Management score.

Social Awareness

I easily connect with others.	I	2	3
I easily sense what others are feeling.	I	2	3
I am a good listener.	I	2	3
I easily see other people's perspectives and points of view.	I	2	3
I get along well with people of diverse backgrounds and cultures.	I	2	3

I have a good sense of the political realities at work in my organization.	I	2	3
I understand the unspoken rules of our organization.	I	2	3
I foster an emotional atmosphere in which people working with our customers can keep those relationships on the right track.	I	2	3
I carefully watch customer satisfaction.	I	2	3
I make myself available to team members, stakeholders, and internal and external customers.	I	2	3

*Add circled items to calculate your total score.
Divide your total by the number of items (10) to get your
Social Awareness score.*

Relationship Management

I easily communicate my vision of the future with others.	I	2	3
I lead by example.	I	2	3
I engage others with a sense of purpose, making work exciting and engaging.	I	2	3
I know how to create buy-in from my team and key stakeholders.	I	2	3
I maintain a strong network of support.	I	2	3
I am concerned with the development and success of those around me.	I	2	3
I coach and mentor others.	I	2	3

I readily give timely and constructive feedback.   I   2   3

I easily recognize when it is time for change.   I   2   3

I challenge the status quo.   I   2   3

I face conflicts directly, acknowledging all sides and
looking for the mutually beneficial solution.   I   2   3

I am a responsible team player.   I   2   3

I work to create close relationships that go beyond
work obligations.   I   2   3

Add circled items to calculate your total score.
Divide your total by the number of items (13) to get
your Relationship Management score.

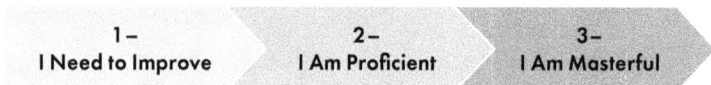

Plot your emotional intelligence scores on this chart:

Self-Awareness

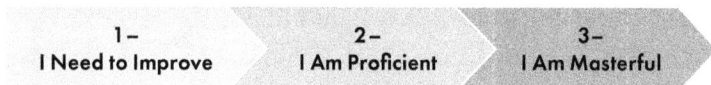

1 – I Need to Improve	2 – I Am Proficient	3 – I Am Masterful

Self-Management

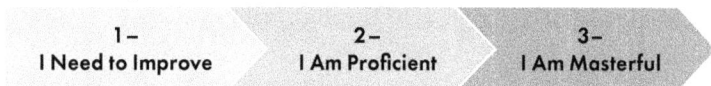

1 – I Need to Improve	2 – I Am Proficient	3 – I Am Masterful

Social Awareness

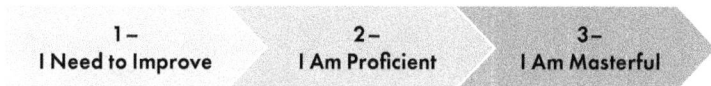

1 – I Need to Improve	2 – I Am Proficient	3 – I Am Masterful

Relationship Management

1 – I Need to Improve	2 – I Am Proficient	3 – I Am Masterful

What do your results tell you about your level of emotional intelligence? How is your level of emotional intelligence impacting your ability to lead others?

Self-Reflection Generates Self-Awareness

Using your results as a starting point, here are some questions to guide your self-reflection and develop your emotional intelligence.

- What is the key lesson learned about your level of self-awareness?
- What triggers negative emotions in you?
- How do you calm yourself?
- What interferes with your ability to motivate yourself?
- What gets in the way of your empathizing with others?
- How does your skill level in social situations impact your performance and advancement?
- What might you do to begin or restart and sustain a practice of self-reflection and discovery to grow self-awareness?
- What are some ways you might grow your capacity to contain the emotions that arise in you and negatively impact your interactions with others?
- Whom would you invite to give you feedback on a regular basis?
- How might mentoring or coaching new Leaders facilitate your growth?

- What would it look like if you were an amazing networker?
- What change to your routine (daily, weekly, monthly) would facilitate you growing your emotional intelligence?
- What can you/will you do to remind yourself of the need to show more empathy and to actually develop a greater ability to demonstrate empathy toward others?

YOU'RE ON THE RIGHT TRACK

A major theme of *Succession* is control. Logan Roy maintains control by keeping everyone around him in a constant state of fear and uncertainty. This makes people easier to control. People aren't engaged. They're not empowered. They aren't activated; they do what they're told, when they're told. Take away the locus of control—in this case, Logan Roy—and the organization crumbles.

Ted Lasso, despite the show's title, isn't about any one person. (As Ted says toward the end of the series finale, "It was never about me.") It's about building a culture. True, Ted is the catalyst for building that culture, but ultimately (spoiler alert!), Ted returns to Kansas while the team he left behind continues to thrive. They've been empowered and activated. Through his leadership, they all cocreated a culture of trust and empowerment.

Ted was never just a Manager. He was always a Coach. He was present and observant, creative and innovative, strategic and purposeful. He engaged people with empathy, warmth, and unconditional positive regard. He was the catalyst; he made the team the locus of control. They owned their situation; they found their own solutions. Because Ted wasn't leading from a position of power, his team didn't need him in order to continue growing and thriving. He taught them everything they needed to know: Believe.

In Part One, I hope we've made the case that the time is now to try coaching for a change. I hope you're still with me. If you've made it this far, you're on the right track. You're a believer. You see the flaws in the command-and-control approach of Logan Roy, and you've seen the strengths in the coaching-forward, "serve to lead" approach of Ted Lasso. I'm even willing to bet that you're already using some of the characteristics of leadership and coaching we discussed in Chapter 1. You're already guided by the coaching mindset as laid out in Chapter 2 and demonstrating and honing the skills here in Chapter 3.

Great work. Let's build on that. When you're ready, Coach, meet me in Part Two.

ARE YOU READY TO COACH?

This self-survey provides you an opportunity to reflect on your ability to empower and activate your team by coaching them. Think about each item on this list. Rate yourself on a scale of one to five, with one meaning this item is an aspiration for you and five meaning the item is true for you all the time.

• I hold regular and frequent coaching conversations with my team members.
• I give timely and direct feedback to help others grow and perform better.
• More often than not, when people bring me their problem, I coach them to find their own solution.
• When coaching, I confirm the what, when, and why of the person's goals.
• I publicly endorse the positive contributions of others.
• When I give feedback, it is based on concrete examples of behavior.
• I follow up with the people I coach to see how they are progressing toward their goals.
• I seek coaching for myself on a regular basis.

If you can answer yes to most of these questions, then you are ready to move on to Part Two. But remember, keep practicing. Great Coaches engage and empower their teams to shape their work and activate them to achieve their best. The characteristics, mindsets, and skills discussed throughout Part One will serve you as you transform yourself into the Great Coach your team wants and needs, whether you're just beginning your leadership journey or are working to fine-tune your approach.

TAKE A BREAK.
HAVE SOME FUN.

My daughter asked me if this book was going to be a pop-up book or have some puzzles in it. She's fun that way. Anyway, because you've made it this far, why not pause and have a little fun break?

Here's a word search to serve as an intermission between Parts 1 and 2. Enjoy!

I	Y	N	D	U	J	F	E	E	D	B	A	C	K
T	N	N	I	L	L	U	M	I	N	A	T	E	D
R	I	X	S	T	R	A	T	E	G	I	C	I	P
S	N	I	V	R	G	Q	C	N	B	X	C	N	R
F	Q	C	H	A	N	G	E	T	O	W	T	N	E
T	U	C	C	P	R	E	T	H	I	N	K	O	S
S	I	C	R	E	A	T	I	V	E	V	I	V	E
E	R	E	M	P	O	W	E	R	D	R	A	A	N
R	Y	B	E	N	D	O	R	S	E	L	M	T	T
V	U	L	E	A	D	E	R	S	H	I	P	I	E
E	M	E	N	G	A	G	E	R	G	O	W	V	C
M	M	L	I	S	T	E	N	I	N	G	J	E	X
C	O	A	C	H	I	N	G	R	E	N	E	W	G
O	B	S	E	R	V	A	N	T	R	E	S	E	T

SERVE	ACTIVATE	INQUIRY
ULTRA	PRESENT	FEEDBACK
LEADERSHIP	OBSERVANT	ENDORSE
CHANGE	CREATIVE	ILLUMINATE
COACHING	INNOVATIVE	RETHINK
ENGAGE	STRATEGIC	RESET
EMPOWER	LISTENING	RENEW

BE A
GR8 COACH

Are your current conversations consistently moving the business forward? Are they helping the team to connect and perform at a high level together?

As you work through Part Two, you may notice a shift in language. In Part One, we talked about coaching another person. Adopting and applying the lessons in this book will make you a better Coach to anyone, anytime, anywhere.

Now it's time to concentrate specifically on your role within your organization. As a Leader, it's your responsibility to engage, empower, and activate your team. Our focus in Part Two is on developing your capacity to coach your team members to feel empowered to shape their work and activate them to achieve their best. From here on out, we're talking about you becoming a GR8 Coach to your *team members*.

As I said in Part One, coaching is more than a good conversation over a cup of coffee. My friend David Isaacs, co-originator of The World Café, says that Leaders design, convene, and host conversations that matter.

Leaders design, convene, and host conversations that matter.

Here in Part Two, I'm going to provide you with frameworks and tools designed to do precisely that.

4

FROM "READY, FIRE, AIM" TO "AIM, ALIGN, ACT"

ECISION-MAKING IS A LEARNING PROCESS. TO make decisions, we learn the facts and choose a course of action. In many organizations today, we make decisions by applying existing information to a situation. This type of cognition is based on the past. It is what W. Brian Arthur of the Santa Fe Institute called "downloading" (e.g., accessing existing information and doing what we did before) in his conversations with Peter Senge, Otto Scharmer, and the other authors of *Presence*. We deploy old models of being, thinking, and doing onto new situations.

We've discussed some of the bad habits that permeate our organizations and teams. Two that are pervasive are our addiction to playing Chief Doer and Expert Problem-Solver and our tendency to race from A to B with a *Ready, Fire, Aim* approach to decision-making. Of those, Ready, Fire, Aim is especially detrimental.

Ready, Fire, Aim has three negative impacts. When we are downloading, racing from point A to point B, we don't take the time to be fully present and open to being informed by our vision of the future or our current reality. Second, our Ready, Fire, Aim habit leaves no room for curiosity or connectivity. The third negative impact builds upon the first two. The lack of openness, curiosity, and connectivity provides no opportunity for creativity or innovation. We generate nothing new. We are simply repeating old patterns.

THE A3 MODEL: AIM, ALIGN, AND ACT

Seeking to help Leaders and teams to Aim before they fire, I devised the A^3 Model. The A^3 Model draws on the work of C. Otto Scharmer of MIT, who has developed a theory of "different levels of perception and change, using the image of a U to distinguish different levels of perceiving reality and different levels of action."[35] Imagine an arrow pointing

---

35 Peter M. Senge, C. Otto Scharmer, Joseph Jaworski, and Betty Sue Flowers, *Presence: Human Purpose and the Field of the Future* (New York: Crown Currency, 2004), 87.

from A (your current state) to B (your desired state). It's a straight line. Theory U takes that line and reshapes it into a U-shaped arrow, visually creating space for more intentional movement through a process that deepens our thinking and conversing before moving to action on our way from A to B. In his book *Theory U: Leading from the Future as It Emerges*, Scharmer describes the five aspects of the U movement as extensions of what happens in all learning processes: Seeing, Sensing, Presencing, Crystallizing, and Realizing.[36]

The three As of the A³ model are: Aim, Align, and Act. We introduce this simplified version of Scharmer's theory to enable easier adoption and wider application of this powerful social technology. Theory U and the A³ model provide a theoretical foundation for the GR8 Coaching Framework and a blueprint for designing coaching conversations that create space for more careful thinking, creativity, and action. Let's look at each element, and then we'll see how A³ lies at the heart of the GR8 Coaching Framework.

Aim

Aiming is an experience of seeing and sensing. If our tendency is to download and race quickly from here to there, do we know where our best "there" lies? Often, we don't, because we're moving too fast. But if we pause to allow an

---

36 C. Otto Scharmer, *Theory U: Leading from the Future as It Emerges*
(Oakland: Berrett-Koehler Publishers, 2009).

inner dialogue or conversation with others, we become present and observe where we want to go and where we are. Then we can Aim at our desired destination. We've taken the first step toward becoming more reflective, less impulsive, and more aligned with both our individual purpose and organizational expectations.

Aiming encourages us to be consciously phenomenological—present and open to both the future state we envision and our current reality, learning from what we are observing. This openness invites inquiry and suspension of our preconceived notions. We can see with fresh eyes. When we Aim to engage other people, we engage with empathy and intentional curiosity, allowing the person or situation to teach us what we need to understand their reality.

Align

Aligning people is one of the ABCs of Leadership. When we talk about Aligning people, we are talking about communicating to ensure alignment around the team's guiding stars: vision, strategy, mission, etc. When we talk about Aligning as a step in the A^3 process, we are talking about the inquiry and creative process that enables a person or people to Align on a way forward.

When we are Aligning, we are engaging in what Scharmer calls Presencing, an experience of intentional curiosity where we can consider multiple courses of action while fully engaged with both past experience and future possibilities.

When we are Aligning, we are creating space for creativity. The more we encourage creativity, the wider the door for innovation through careful and strategic thinking opens. We create an opportunity for something (or someone) to move from one state of being to another. In those moments we begin to behave differently, opening up to something not previously imagined coming into being.

By taking time to Align, we engage our imaginations and consider all options. We foster a dialogue with ourselves or with others to consider the advantages and disadvantages of each course of action open to us. If we continue to be consciously phenomenological in our thinking and attitude, the possibilities will multiply. By reflecting before jumping into action, we not only open the door to more possibilities, we also reduce the likelihood of costly missteps as we move to execute our plans with greater alignment.

We are always moving. The first question is whether or not all that activity is aligned with any organizational strategy and sense of purpose. The next question is: are we aiming in the right direction?

Act

Acting is an experience of crystallizing and realizing. Acting involves laying out a strategy and making plans to move quickly, strategically, and with alignment. We put the pieces together, choose the best course of action, chart it out, and start acting strategically and with a sense of purpose.

THE GR8 COACHING FRAMEWORK

The GR8 Coaching Framework will help you successfully complete the Aim-Align-Act triad. The Framework is a conversation design and a coaching tool intended to help you fight back against the Ready, Fire, Aim habit and the addiction to playing Chief Doer and Expert Problem-Solver in order to have conversations that matter with your team members. Here's what happens when you use the GR8 Coaching Framework:

- You have no choice but to be present and observant, creative and innovative, and strategic and purposeful.

- You can't help but embrace the coaching mindset while demonstrating and developing your coaching skill set.

- You will engage your team members and empower them to activate and achieve their objective.

- These coaching conversations will solve pressing problems, help your team members capitalize on adjacent opportunities, and build individual capacity— all of which will enable positive transformation and move your organization forward. Using the GR8 Coaching Framework, you're following the A^3 model and creating a U-shaped experience for someone. By doing so, you're also practicing and reinforcing the

ABCs of Leadership: Aligning people, Building bench strength, and Coordinating action.

Just like anything, you must practice using this framework for it to work. Years ago, when 1 was training for my first triathlon, 1 worked with a Coach to help me prepare for the swimming segment. 1 knew how to swim, but triathlons require a different technique. He taught me all kinds of things, from breathing, to arm position, to the way 1 kicked my legs. At first, it was overwhelming to keep all this information in mind while also just swimming. But eventually, 1 no longer had to consciously think about my Coach's instructions because 1 had internalized them.

The same is true of coaching using the GR8 Coaching Framework. When you're first starting out, you're thinking about the process. That's good; it means you're acting with intention. Then, over time, coaching will become more natural and intuitive, informed by your increased knowledge, developed skills, and gained experience. You'll automatically help people resolve their situations and move themselves forward in a positive way.

You'll remember the eight powerful questions from the GR8 Coaching Framework without any effort. Let's take a look.

GR8 Coaching Questions

1. Get Started: What's going on? Connect and explore the person's situation.

2. Get Focused: What's the best possible outcome? Zero in on the highest intent.

3. Get Real: What's in your way? Shine a light on the barriers to success—both external and internal.

4. Get Serious: What absolutely must happen? Identify what absolutely has to occur for the person to declare success.

5. Get Creative: What are your options? Generate multiple options to achieve success.

6. Get Strategic: How does each option get you closer to your best possible outcome? Weigh each option and evaluate each possible course of action.

7. Get Organized: What will you do? Formulate a plan for moving forward.

8. Get Going: What's the simplest, best next step? Commit to the simplest, best next step.

As you move through the questions in the GR8 Coaching Framework, you will naturally move your coaching conversations from idea to action—anchored by an intentional, expansive framework for decision-making.

That's the beauty of the A^3 model: it formalizes behaviors we already know to be successful. To fully understand how this works, in the next three chapters, we'll take a deep dive into the eight questions that form the backbone of the GR8 Coaching Framework:

GR8 COACHING FRAMEWORK

1. **GET STARTED:** What's going on?

2. **GET FOCUSED:** What's the best possible outcome?

3. **GET REAL:** What's in your way?

4. **GET SERIOUS:** What absolutely must happen?

5. **GET CREATIVE:** What are your options?

6. **GET STRATEGIC:** How does each option get you closer to your best possible outcome?

7. **GET ORGANIZED:** What will you do?

8. **GET GOING:** What's the simplest, best next step? Commit to the simplest, best next step.

- Chapter 5: **Aiming** (Questions 1–3). These questions help your team member be present and observant of their situation.
- Chapter 6: **Aligning** (Questions 4–6). These questions invite your team member to open to different possibilities to address their situation.
- Chapter 7: **Acting** (Questions 7–8). These questions move your team member to be strategic and purposeful in laying out their way forward.

As you begin practicing the questions outlined in the following chapters, you might find that they feel stilted or prescriptive at first. Think of these questions as training wheels, not an immutable formula. Following these questions word for word *will* lead you and your team to the outcomes you're looking for, but there's always space for improvisation once you've grokked the process.

As you get more comfortable with the GR8 Coaching Framework, you will learn to make these questions your own. As long as you're designing conversations that are expansive, open-ended, and focused on uncovering the next right step without any prescriptive or preconceived notions of how to proceed, then you are most likely coaching effectively. The questions will reveal whether you're doing precisely that.

When Leaders we work with first start with the GR8 Coaching Framework, they often realize that although they thought they were coaching effectively, in reality, they'd been coaching the problem rather than the person, unconsciously trying to force the situation from point A to point B and commanding rather than supporting the person they were supposed to be leading.

So, even if you don't fully understand why you should follow the GR8 Coaching Framework or how the questions work to shape an effective coaching experience, why not give it a try? I'm confident that if you do, you will quickly come to see their value. Remember, sometimes action leads to insight.

And with that said, let's get started.

5

AIM

I KNEW A CHIEF MARKETING OFFICER (CMO) WHO WAS a serial rusher. No planning, no self-reflection, no consideration for how his actions fit in with the rest of the organization's vision. He was a real Ready, Fire, Aim guy. In his mind, he knew everything.

When confronted with a problem, he would apply the same old answer to new questions. He would go to the file drawer in his brain, pull out an idea that had worked previously, dust it off, change the colors, and apply it to the new situation, no matter how bad the fit. He'd built a playbook of these ideas in the early years of his career and never bothered to update it.

Sometimes, going back to the old file drawer would work for him. More often, however, he'd find himself making the same mistakes over and over again.

One day, a new Leader came into the organization, to whom the CMO now reported. The new Leader expected the CMO to change things up in terms of how he approached his work, collaborated with peers, and managed his team, and he couldn't do it. Ninety days later, the Leader had managed the CMO out of his job.

I don't mean to pick on this person. In truth, I see this same pattern of behavior frequently among Leaders. They race to solutions, make quick judgments, and copy and paste old approaches. When they reach a point where they need to change or develop a new skill, they're done. They cannot or will not Aim before they fire.

In this chapter, you'll learn how the GR8 Coaching Framework can help you break this habit—for yourself and the people you lead. By coaching your team members to first take Aim before Acting, you will better position both yourself and your team to take meaningful action and create positive transformation for your organization.

In truth, the three Aiming questions explored in this chapter are valuable whether you're too quick to copy/paste an old solution to a new problem or you suffer from what is frequently called *analysis paralysis*: the tendency to overthink a problem in lieu of action. Whatever the case, the Aiming questions help you Coach your team member to get fully present, identify their highest intent, and thoroughly examine what's in their way.

PRACTICE SAFE COACHING

Before we dive into our three Aiming questions, let's take a moment to discuss a couple of essential best practices. Remembering these will help keep you safe while coaching, creating an environment that empowers your team member to Aim, Align, and Act.

Coaching Is Not Therapy

Many years ago, I was sitting on a panel at a coaching conference. Almost the entire audience was professional Coaches. When the moderator asked me what I thought about coaching, I said, "I think coaching has great potential. At the moment, I see a lot of Coaches performing very bad therapy without a license."

The comment got a few laughs, but the point was serious. I've practiced as both a therapist and a Coach, and I can say definitively that they are not the same thing.

So, repeat after me: "I am not a therapist."

The Aiming conversation should not be a big exploration of your team member's childhood. You aren't asking about their unconscious traumatic motivations. You're there to support them in navigating a work situation.

To do that, your job is to learn what's going on for them at work so that you can Coach them, not therapize and solve their problems. Follow the GR8 Coaching Framework, and you'll save yourself the mistake of practicing bad therapy without a license. That's not what you're there for. The GR8 Coaching Framework keeps you on course. You're facilitating their thinking, their problem-solving and creative solutioning, and their taking steps toward their goals.

Listen and Validate

You're also not there to judge. As you listen to your team member's answers, your role is not to pass judgment about whether your team member is doing something bad or good. You're looking for objective data, not subjective opinion. Be present and observant. Connect and empathize. They're sharing their current experience, who they are, and what they're bringing to the coaching conversation.

If you feel yourself jumping into rescuer mode, pause, listen, and reflect back and validate what you're hearing. Their experience is theirs. That's enough to make it legitimate. Often, if someone I'm coaching is unburdening themselves of quite a lot, I'll simply say, "Wow, that's a lot. You're carrying all of that. You have a lot going on." Acknowledging their experience is the first step to finding out what's most important in the sea of information you've just heard.

Take Your Time

As you walk into any coaching conversation, set aside any expectations of how long it should take. It takes as long as it takes. Sometimes you can get through all eight questions in fifteen minutes, while other times you will spend an hour just on the first question or two. The full eight questions could take ten minutes or ten weeks, depending on the complexity of the situation, the team member's level of self-awareness, and whether they've done any prep work.

Similarly, your own responsibility to the conversation will also impact its length. Sometimes you will need to share a fair amount of feedback, while other times you and your team member will already be on the same page. Sometimes, you will need to dig in with your team member to focus on two or three barriers that they must solve for in order to achieve their desired outcome.

That said, as your relationship develops and deepens over a series of coaching conversations, you can often work through the framework much more quickly. You and your team member will both be familiar with the framework and know how the other person works. They may even start asking themselves these questions to problem-solve on their own between coaching sessions. Whatever the case, your objective at the outset of every conversation is the same: to engage your team members and empower them to Aim, Align, and Act to shape their work and achieve their best.

EXPLORING THE GR8 COACHING FRAMEWORK

With these guardrails above in place, you're ready to explore the GR8 Coaching Framework. Let's go.

1. GET STARTED

What's Going On?

We all have a lot going on. Any coaching session needs a jumping-off point. When kicking off a coaching conversation, your goal is to get present with your team member. You need your team member to catch you up since the last time you spoke. "What's going on?" is an invitation to share the things that are front of mind for your team member. It immediately moves you past small talk.

Their job is to share their current experience. Your job as Coach is to try to understand. As they convey what's going on, you might need to ask some follow-ups for clarification. Here are a couple of my favorites:

- What's keeping you up at night?
- What's currently your biggest concern?

However you ask it, the Get Started question allows your team member to get things out of their heads. I know that when I'm dealing with multiple challenges, I begin to swirl. Talking with my Coach, who asks me, "What's going on?" allows me to get it out and take a look at it, and it empowers me to decide what's important and what's not, which leads me right into the next question.

GR8 COACH CHECKPOINT:
NO SOLVING ALLOWED

This first question is a potential landmine. As you hear your team member sharing what's going on, your first instinct may be to jump to solution mode. Remember, you're coaching the person, not the problem. It'll take all your emotional self-management chops to fight the urge to play Expert Problem-Solver here.

One reason this is critically important is that the problem your team member is sharing with you may not be the real problem. More times than not, the problem they describe is actually a symptom of another deeper problem. Don't get sucked into solving the wrong problem. Be strong. Use the Force, Luke!

2. GET FOCUSED

What's the Best Possible Outcome?

The first of the GR8 Coaching questions is designed to get your team member to share their current state and presenting issues. This second question is intended to narrow down what you'll be focusing on during this coaching session. To do that, ask, "What's the best possible outcome?"

As you work through this question, here are two things to keep in mind.

Prioritize

Often, your team member will list multiple issues in response to the Get Started question—sometimes twenty or more. Even if your team member infodumps a laundry list of issues, those issues can't all be of equal importance or urgency. Further, if your team member tends to rush to a solution without sifting through their priorities, they might end up solving the wrong problem, taking on something that isn't their responsibility, or treating a symptom rather than the actual problem. The Get Focused question helps your team member prioritize in real time. The question enables them to get clear on what is truly important, what is less important, and what is merely a distraction.

For example, I once asked a Leader, "What's going on?" and he shared that a member of his team was leaving to go work in another part of the organization. "Okay, what's the best possible outcome?" I asked.

"I would have a replacement in place within ninety days," he said. That was an essential piece of information—and his response clearly indicated that this issue was more important than some of the other ideas swirling in his mind. He had identified a clear need with an urgent timeline. By walking him through the GR8 Coaching Framework, we were able to sort his priorities and lay out an actionable plan to move forward.

If you create the space to pause and reflect, most people will intuitively identify their priorities. Left to their own devices, though, they're likely to either race to the first thing that seems like a solution or retreat into analysis paralysis. Asking them to picture the best possible outcome helps to cut through those unproductive habits and identify the most pressing need.

If someone stalls out at this question, here's where you get to shine as a Coach. Typically, in these situations, I'll say something along the lines of: "So you've talked about twenty things that are going on right now that you say require your attention. What's the best possible outcome at the end of this quarter? What are we celebrating? It's only ninety days, and you can't do it all. So, what are the top three or four things you absolutely must do yourself and can't delay or delegate?" When confronted with the additional restriction of time—in this case, ninety days—most people are able to make an informed choice and begin to activate on that choice.

Is That Yours?

Sometimes, even when you've encouraged your team member to prioritize, they'll resist. In that case, you can come at it from a different angle. For each task that team member has listed out, ask, "Is that truly your work?" Some people worry about everything but the kitchen sink, and the issues they lay on the table aren't their responsibility. You're there to help them make that distinction. As Coach, you help them pressure test their choices.

In my experience, many Leaders spend as much as 25 percent of their time doing work that belongs to one of their direct reports. Often, they know they shouldn't be doing the work, but they do it anyway as a way to: (1) avoid feeling discomfort; (2) avoid a hard conversation; or (3) do the work faster and/or the way they want it.

For instance, I had a conversation with a Leader who had very clear annual performance objectives (APOs). If he didn't meet those objectives, he wouldn't receive his full bonus. Yet he was spending an inordinate amount of time on a couple of tasks that had no impact on his APOs. Through coaching, he was able to get clear and refocus.

"What's the best possible outcome?" I asked.

"I deliver on my APOs and get my full bonus," he replied.

If, like my client, you're doing work that isn't moving the needle for your organization, it's time to stop. Focus on your own work and keep your team focused on prioritizing their tasks. Effective leadership requires knowing how to delegate, not scrambling to take on problems that don't even belong to you. That's the old, usual, and ordinary way. You're shifting from Manager to Coach.

This is what I mean when I say that the GR8 Coaching

Framework can help both your team members and you. In fact, for many of my coaching clients, the Get Focused question evokes a profound moment of clarity, allowing them to realize they're doing a ton of work they shouldn't be doing.

GR8 COACH CHECKPOINT: STAY IN YOUR LANE

As a Coach, you're a thinking partner. Your inquiry is guiding your team member through a process that begins with being present to their current situation and finding the signal in the noise. The start of any GR8 Coaching conversation offers your team member the chance to both recalibrate and step into fuller accountability. They own their current state and are declaring their desired future state. Your ability to stay present and fight the urge to jump into problem-solving mode is laying the foundation for your team member to explore how they're on track or off in realizing their best possible outcome as the coaching conversation continues. Stay in your lane.

And speaking of getting back on track, that leads us to our next question.

3. GET REAL

What's in Your Way?

Your team member has shared what's front of mind for them and focused on their best possible outcome. An idea of the best possible outcome is the starting point. Now it's time to Get Real, to take a careful look at what might be in their way. The GR8 Question to prompt that work is "What's in your way?" In other words, "What are the barriers to your achieving that best possible outcome we just talked about?"

External Barriers

When asked what's in their way, most people will start by listing external obstacles. Your team member will likely do the same. For instance, they may tell you that another team is behind on a deliverable that is vital to their work, or a particular process is broken, or someone on another team is blocking their path. Whatever the reasons, allow them to identify all the external barriers in their way.

Symptom or Problem?

Your team member is sharing their truth. The barriers they share are real for them. Coaching them to see and examine all the external barriers is a critical step in their problem-solving process. As your team member's Coach, you want to help them determine whether the problem they're describing isn't actually a symptom of another, perhaps deeper, problem. For each identified barrier, ask, "Is this the real problem or a symptom of something else?" In a way, you're helping them to do some root cause analysis—looking for the cause of problems to suggest possible solutions.

Internal Barriers

Not all barriers are external. Sometimes, we get in our own way. Getting real means looking at how our beliefs, behaviors, habits, or practices hinder our ability to succeed. A great Get Real follow-up is "How are you contributing to the status quo?" In Marshall Goldsmith's terrific book *What Got You Here Won't Get You There*, he lays out twenty-one ways we get in our own way and hold ourselves back. As one of the Coaches on my team likes to put it, "How are you sabotaging yourself unconsciously?"

The Gift of Feedback

When you ask the Get Real question, you give your team member an opportunity to reflect on their role in creating their situation. Maybe the barrier is simply an exterior one. If it is, you can move on. If it isn't, developing self-awareness of how we are cocreators of our shared experiences is a gift. So, what do you do if you believe your team member is getting in their own way? You have to give them a gift—the gift of feedback.

We'll discuss feedback again in a later chapter. For now, know that getting real with your team member may require you to give them some feedback. Even in the context of a coaching conversation, it's best to ask permission before giving feedback. Say, "We've laid out some things in your way. I think there's something we haven't touched on. Can I give you some feedback?"

In Chapter 3, we discussed two types of feedback: endorsements and illuminations. Endorsements are specific callouts of an observed behavior or action that had a positive impact.

Endorsements are specific callouts of an observed behavior or action that had a positive impact.

As you're getting real with your team member, you'll likely have an illumination to share. There will be times when you have to give what might be called negative or constructive feedback, an illumination. You are shining a light on a behavior that the person may not realize is counterproductive and detracting from their intended impact.

All behavior has meaning. We only do things if we believe that we are getting something out of it. If someone focuses on tasks other than the work directly tied to their APOs and bonus, why? What are they getting out of that? Does it give them a rush? Is it more exciting? Is it a way of avoiding something?

Illuminating a self-limiting behavior is a powerful gift. Your feedback empowers your team member to consider how their thought process and behaviors contribute to the status quo. How are they getting in their own way? How aware are they of how they're getting in their own way? You'll be surprised at what you and your team member might uncover.

When I was leading a company and a team for the first time, my Coach would ask me, "What's going on?" I'd offer up a list of all the different business aspects, projects, and team responsibilities I was working on. His version of the Get Focused question was "What are you trying to achieve?" Then, he'd ask a Get Real question: "How are you contributing to the status quo?"

Just like many of the people I coach, I wasn't fully aware of how I was contributing to the status quo. My Coach had a pretty good idea—but he wanted me to figure it out for myself.

One day, he said to me, "Who tells Shaq to sit down?" (This was back when basketball legend Shaquille O'Neal still played for the Los Angeles Lakers.)

"No one tells Shaq to sit down," I said. "If Shaq wants to play, he's in the game. If Shaq wants to sit down, he'll tell the Coach he's tired and needs a break. Otherwise, Shaq is on the court."

"Can I give you some feedback? You are Shaq, and you are sitting," he said. Then, without missing a beat, he asked, "Why are you sitting?"

Oof.

My team knew that I was running the company, but I wasn't showing up as a Leader. I wasn't embracing my role as the Shaq of my company. I was holding back, keeping myself on the bench in many situations when I should have been on the court. My Coach saw this, and he gave me just the prodding I needed to see it too. He shared a valuable illumination.

But again, notice what my Coach didn't do. He didn't play therapist. He didn't ask about my repressed internal motivations. He didn't try to analyze me. He just pointed out what I was doing and helped me see clearly how it undermined what I said I wanted to achieve. By getting real with me and making the space for me to consider how I was holding myself back, my Coach helped me see how my internal barriers were in part a symptom of how I was setting about to do my work.

Even after that realization, I still had more work to do, but getting real shook me loose and set me on the right path. It provided me with essential illumination. In my subsequent work as a Coach, I've often used a version of the Shaq analogy to ask people how they're holding themselves back and need help taking themselves off the bench. Their behavior has meaning. It's a behavior that they adopted because it served them at some point, even though it wasn't working anymore. To achieve what we want to achieve, we must Align our behavior with our real goals. Your job as a Coach isn't to Align that behavior yourself, but rather to point out misalignments and help people see how it does and doesn't serve what they say they want to do.

Getting real about external and internal barriers sets up a choice: What do you want to do about it?

Getting real about external and internal barriers sets up a choice: What do you want to do about it?

GR8 COACH CHECKPOINT:
AIM *BEFORE* YOU FIRE

By this point in your coaching conversation, you and your team member have identified everything going on, and of all that's going on, focused on their best possible outcomes. The Get Real questions and follow-ups are an examination of the reasons or obstacles—real or imagined, external, or internal—impacting your team member's ability to achieve their desired outcomes. In the Get Started, Get Focused, and Get Real questions, you have helped them begin to shift from Ready, Fire, Aim to Aim, Align, Act. Your coaching is producing change.

Having taken time to Aim before we fire, our coaching conversation shifts into creative mode and Aligning on the best option for moving forward in a strategic and purposeful way. The next few questions in the GR8 Coaching Framework help you create space for your team member to be creative and strategic in mapping out a course of action that sets them on a path to success.

6

ALIGN

A LIGNING IS ABOUT DISRUPTING THE STATUS quo. Doing what you did last time isn't always good enough. By getting serious, getting creative, and getting strategic, you and your team member will arrive at more innovative, more creative, and more effective solutions.

But did you know that nearly 95 percent of our decision-making occurs in our subconscious minds? According to research led by Chun Siong Soon, our brains are already subconsciously prepared to make a decision before we consciously make it.[37] How can our subconscious do this?

---

37 Chun Siong Soon et al., "Unconscious determinants of free decisions in the human brain," *Nature Neuroscience* 11 (2008): 543–545, https://doi.org/10.1038/nn.2112.

Because of the way our brains access information. According to research by Joel L. Voss and Ken A. Paller, the brain accesses stored information accumulated over a lifetime.[38] It then uses this information to make decisions quickly—so fast that we make the decision before we are conscious of making it.

This is a remarkable feat of biology, but it's not without consequences. When we base our decisions solely on what we've experienced in the past, it not only prevents us from seeing the present decision clearly, but it subverts our ability to understand the consequences.

What we want to do is exactly the opposite—we want to support people to see the present decision clearly and understand its consequences. After all, the subtitle of this book is *How to Engage, Empower, and Activate People*. That's the core of your work as a Leader. We empower people when we expect them to own their situation and find their own solutions. We coach the person, not the problem. That, in turn, is activating. By engaging your team members as a Coach, you empower them to decide what must happen, what they will do to achieve their best possible outcome, and how to address any barriers in their way. Helping them Align on the optimal way forward requires careful, conscious thinking— and careful, conscious thinking isn't the default setting for

38 Joel L. Voss and Ken A. Paller, "An electrophysiological signature of unconscious recognition memory," *Nature Neuroscience* 12 (2009): 349–355, https://doi.org/10.1038/nn.2260.

most of us. When you engage as a Coach, you help your team member overcome this fact.

The GR8 Coaching Framework's Aligning questions promote careful thinking. Your coaching inquiry short-circuits our first instinct to download what we did last time and the time before in this new situation. You help someone switch off the autopilot and fight the Ready, Fire, Aim urge. You move decision-making from a subconscious to a conscious act.

Careful thinking involves being able to encounter confusion, hold multiple pieces of information in our memories at any given moment, analyze each piece of information, and understand the relationship among all that information to lessen the confusion. Careful thinking also involves generating and considering new and creative opportunities to address challenges and to prioritize based on strategic value.

Here are some signs you (or the person you are coaching) are thinking carefully:

- You anticipate change and are proactive in addressing potential objections and barriers.
- You question your own assumptions as part of your decision-making process.
- You see the underlying patterns that cause problems.
- You consider the higher intent when making decisions and prioritizing actions.
- You consider, compare, and contrast multiple options and their possible outcomes before making a decision.

- You're good at prioritization.
- You consider other people's perspectives and points of view as part of your decision-making process.
- You're open to learning new things.

If you're seeking to enable the positive transformation of another person through coaching, you want to help that person think carefully. Your intention and theirs is to be present and observant in order to be creative and innovative so they can act strategically and purposefully. To empower your team members—these future leaders who will follow your example as they step into and grow their own leadership—you must create the right environment, a carefully cultivated space for introspection and insight that produces positive change for the person and their situation.

CREATE SPACE

The first step for creating such an environment is simple: Slow down. Don't rush through the ideation process these questions generate. You are creating the space to let the best ideas take root and grow. In a discussion on thinking to create change with the authors of *Presence*, Peter Senge, Otto Scharmer, Joseph Jaworski, and Betty Sue Flowers, W. Brian Arthur put it this way:

> In this country, managers think that a fast decision is what counts. If the situation is new, slowing down is

necessary. Slow down. Observe. Position yourself. Then act fast and with a natural flow that comes from the inner knowing. You have to slow down long enough to really see what's needed. With a freshness of vision, you have the possibility of a freshness of action, and the overall response on a collective level can be much quicker than trying to implement hasty decisions that aren't compelling to people.[39]

Aligning is a creative dance—an expansive part of the process that allows your team member to identify and evaluate options for moving forward. Something has to happen. Something different has to happen. Something new has to happen. That's what change is all about: opening up to greater possibilities and then making those possibilities the new reality. The Aligning phase of our coaching is where the past and future intersect. In the parlance of Arthur, we are "allowing inner knowing to emerge."

This isn't always an easy or natural thing to do. As Arthur pointed out, "freshness of vision" and "freshness of action" rarely happen on their own. Don't underestimate the powerful tendency we have to rush to the obvious solution rather than draw out the best solution. We do that when we aren't rushed or stressed. When you factor in deadlines, fire drills,

---

39   Peter M. Senge, C. Otto Scharmer, Joseph Jaworski, and Betty Sue Flowers, *Presence: Human Purpose and the Field of the Future* (New York: Crown Currency, 2004).

and break-ins from our boss or our boss's boss, our predilection for Ready, Fire, Aim gets dialed up to eleven. The Aligning questions are designed to short-circuit that tendency so that you and your team member can approach their goals and challenges with greater care. They are the core of the GR8 Coaching Framework.

Through the Aligning questions, you and your team member will carefully lay out possible options, consider each one, challenge underlying assumptions, and then evaluate the implications of each option.

GR8 COACH CHECKPOINT:
STAY CURIOUS AND TAKE YOUR TIME

The Aligning questions keep you honest. You're helping someone with their thinking, problem-solving, and decision-making. Depending on the situation, you're helping your team member to slow down, speed up, or broaden or deepen their thinking so they can choose the best option from the full spectrum of possibilities in a creative, careful, and considered way. In other words, you're saving them from locking in on the first idea that pops into their head.

To coach someone toward creative, careful, and considered thinking, you must also practice creative, careful, and considered thinking. If you're leading someone toward the option that immediately stood out to you, you're merely downloading an old solution and applying it to a new coaching conversation. To avoid that pitfall, remember the mindsets, skills, and behaviors we discussed in Part One:

You're coaching your team member to find their optimal solution, not the obvious solution.

Look to learn. You may have some ideas of your own (all of which you will keep to yourself), but you will develop a more nuanced appreciation for your team member by listening and asking questions.

Give your team member the time, space, and permission to be creative.

4. GET SERIOUS

What Absolutely Must Happen?

With our first three GR8 Questions, we took Aim at the current reality, established a vision of the future, and generated an understanding of the internal and external obstacles in the way of that future. You have an idea of the best possible outcome and have done an honest assessment of what's in the way. As coaching shifts to Aligning, it's time to Get

Serious, to ask the question: to achieve that outcome and remove the barriers, what absolutely must happen?

I like the Get Serious question because it gets down to brass tacks, establishes accountability, and forces your team member to prioritize. This is a big deal. In my experience, one of the key factors that hold many organizations, teams, and Leaders back is their inability to radically prioritize. Most Leaders and teams have a significant backlog of work that is deemed important and needs a person or group to take it on and complete it. Most people and teams have a hard time sorting through their backlog, prioritizing the work, and focusing on those things that are most pressing. Radical prioritization forces us to focus only on the most important thing, the thing that must happen right now because it is both important and urgent.

Let's say that, during the Aiming questions, you and your team member determined that one of the best possible outcomes is that your team member has hired and onboarded a new project manager by the end of the quarter. You ask them, "To achieve this outcome, what absolutely must happen?"

They might reply, "The requisition needs to be opened. Interviews will need to be scheduled. We'll need to make an offer. The onboarding process will need to be designed."

In another scenario, one of your team member's best possible outcomes is that she has generated consensus for an important initiative by the end of the year. A big barrier is that her relationships with a couple of her peers are not strong at the moment.

Again, you ask, "To achieve this outcome, what absolutely must happen?"

She might reply, "I'll need to schedule some meetings to invite my peers into the work. Before that, I probably need to reengage some of them to check on our relationship, get feedback, and invite them to collaborate in a different way."

I Like Ike

If you or your team member need help with radical prioritization, I recommend the Eisenhower Matrix. The Eisenhower Matrix, made popular by Stephen Covey in *The Seven Habits of Highly Effective People*, is a tool for prioritizing tasks by urgency and importance. Covey's model for this prioritization matrix comes from its namesake, former President Dwight D. Eisenhower, who, in a 1954 speech, said, "I have two kinds of problems, the urgent and the important. The urgent are not important, and the important are never urgent."

	URGENT	NOT URGENT
IMPORTANT	Do: Tasks with deadlines or consequences	Schedule: Tasks with unclear deadlines that contribute to long-term success
NOT IMPORTANT	Delegate: Tasks that must be done but don't require you	Delete: Distractions and unnecessary tasks

When your team member relates what's going on and shares their best possible outcome, they are talking about something immediate. Their best possible outcome has a time component, usually within the current quarter. The Eisenhower Matrix can help your team member get serious about what's truly important and urgent, making it a great tool for Aligning.

When I'm coaching busy executives, for instance, I often work with them to set their target outcomes, first for the year and then for each quarter. When shaping their work for the year, most of them show me a list of twenty or more things that "absolutely" must happen. All twenty items might be important, but they can't all be urgent. If everything is urgent, then nothing is urgent.

Besides, even if every one of those twenty items was equally important, none of these executives would ever be able to get all of them done. Even if they managed to find space on their calendar, their calendar would fight back. Why? Because everyone needs space on their calendar for the inevitable break-ins and requests for their time that fall outside their priorities. And that goes double for Leaders and executives, who need space and flexibility in order to not totally blow up their quarterly Tactical Action Plan.

Knowing this, I ask the Leaders I coach to Get Serious and probe deeper:

- Do all twenty really need to happen?

- Let's say you can't do all twenty, only ten. Which ten must absolutely happen?
- Now what if you could only do five?

Through this intentional process, we separate the true must-haves from the nice-to-haves. If I'm working with someone on prioritizing their next ninety days, then we work to get even clearer—from five goals down to three. To do that, what absolutely must happen?

Through this process, not only do these executives achieve tremendous clarity, but they also become far more willing to let go of their nice-to-have goals for the upcoming year or quarter. Yes, those goals might still be important, but they aren't as important or urgent when compared to their other to-dos. And they can always be delegated. The power of the Get Serious question is its gift of intentionality. The question and the thinking it provokes enable greater attention management and thereby better time and calendar management.

By getting serious with your team member, you remind them that they have the power to choose. No one's telling them to do an impossible number of things or which things to let go of. They know their priorities, and they make the plan. And with this clarity of intention, they feel empowered to let less urgent tasks go.

If you're unaccustomed to operating in this way, it can feel terrifying at first. However, I've found it's far preferable to feeling like you need to carry everything everywhere all at once.

5. GET CREATIVE

What Are Your Options?

Creativity is often associated with artists, writers, and designers, but it is a vital skill for Leaders as well. When we coach team members to approach decision-making creatively, we open up a world of possibilities that traditional methods might overlook.

Now that your team member is dialed in on what absolutely must happen, it's time to help them imagine the different ways to make those things happen. To open this part of the conversation, ask, "What are your options?" By considering multiple options, your team member is tapping into creativity that can unlock innovative solutions. Considering multiple options is at the heart of creative decision-making. It involves exploring various possibilities and evaluating their potential benefits and drawbacks. This approach can lead to more innovative and effective solutions.

"What are your options?" is an invitation to perform creative work. As a Coach, your job during this part of the conversation is to prevent your team member from latching onto any preconceived notion or belief. The goal is to foster expansive thinking, to push your team member to get more careful and creative in their thinking, and to help them see there's always more than one way to achieve the best possible outcome.

To do this, it's important to distinguish between outcomes and tasks. For instance, imagine I want to get from San Diego to New York by March 13. That's my best possible outcome, and it absolutely must happen. To achieve that outcome, I have many options available to me. I could hitchhike, take a road trip, ride a train, book a flight, or sail south around Cape Horn and back up north to New York. Any one of those methods would represent the big-picture task, with tons of smaller to-dos within them.

But which method is the right method? The default option would be to book the flight—and that very well may be the case. However, it's important to note that that option assumes expediency is the most important variable. Perhaps flexibility and sightseeing are really important to me, in which case the road trip might be the best option. Or, if I want to be a modern Ferdinand Magellan, then perhaps I'll leave a few months early and sail around South America.

The point is, when considering options, coach your team member not to mix up the outcome with the method. If, at the outset of this conversation, your team member blurts out, "I must book a plane ticket for March 13," then they're jumping ahead and foreclosing other, potentially better (or at least more interesting) options. In that case, encourage them to mark that idea down, set it aside, and continue to think of other options.

Remember, with this question, we are trying to short-circuit the Ready, Fire, Aim habit and encourage more careful and creative thinking. Before your team member decides what they *will* do, they have to consider what they *might* do.

GR8 COACH CHECKPOINT:
THEIR OPTIONS, NOT YOURS

If you're like me and many of the Leaders I coach, your Expert Problem-Solver impulse will flare up quite a bit during the Get Creative phase.

It's natural to feel an urge to jump in with your own answers—or worse, to offer your opinion on what seems like the best answer. You're a good problem-solver, after all, and you're just trying to be helpful, right?

Not so fast.

Remember the person you're coaching. You're here to support them in coming up with their own solution. It's not your job to provide the answers.

Yes, the brainstorming phase is exciting. Yes, you might have some fantastic ideas rattling around in your head. And yes, your team member may be overlooking something when they're first generating and evaluating options. But it's imperative that you contain your excitement so that your team member can be their own problem-solver.

To do that, stick with inquiry. Keep asking questions until the person you're coaching has a wealth of strong options on the table.

By doing this, you create the space for two things to happen. First, your team member remains engaged in the problem and empowered to find their own solutions. Second, you avoid putting your thumb on the scale and guiding the conversation toward a suboptimal solution.

Remember, as the Leader, what you say has extra weight. Your team member is going to want to please you. Even if you think you're just brainstorming, your team member will rightly assume that you wouldn't offer a suggestion that you wouldn't want to do yourself. As a result, they'll think, "My boss likes this option—I should probably go along with it." The very thought is disempowering.

6. GET STRATEGIC

How Does Each Option Get You Closer to Your Best Possible Outcome?

Having identified the options, it's time to get strategic. Ask, "How does each option get you closer to your best possible outcome?" Given all the possibilities, what is the best course of action? Your coaching here helps your team member evaluate the efficacy of each option they identified.

Let's say your team member needs to fill a crucial sales role. The options you brainstormed include the following:

- Delegate hiring to an external firm.
- Promote from within.
- Divide the work among existing roles.

Those are three strong, viable options. But how does each option get your team member closer to their target outcome? Which option will be most effective in filling that sales role? What assumptions are behind each option? What are the implications associated with following through on each option?

To help your team member select their preferred option, remember these key things:

- "Easiest" and "best" are not always the same. In fact, they usually aren't.
- Avoid downloading an old solution onto a new situation. It might work, but it doesn't mean it will work well.
- When it comes to problem-solving, the first thought is not always the optimal solution. It's merely the obvious one.

With these guardrails in place, your team member can examine all the options and arrive at an informed decision. For each option they surface, ask them whether that choice seems good, bad, or okay. How can they tell? If appropriate, ask, "What are you avoiding with this option?" The Stoics say the obstacle is the way, and the only way is through. Is a given option a workaround, or is it truly solving for something?

If, after considering every option, the old solution is still objectively the best strategy moving forward, then go ahead and pencil it in. In the Acting questions in the next chapter, your team member will have the opportunity to set their plan in ink.

GR8 COACH CHECKPOINT:
WHAT IF THE OPTIONS AREN'T GOOD?

In the fourth season of *True Detective*, Jodi Foster plays the chief of police in the fictional town of Ennis, Alaska. Throughout the season, she takes one of the officers under her wing, coaching him to better define the problem they're trying to solve by reconsidering the core issue at hand. When he gets offtrack, she says, "You're asking the wrong question. Ask again."

As a Coach, if you have an option in your head and your team member isn't getting to it, then the next step isn't to tell them the answer. It's to ask better questions to broaden your team member's thinking and take the conversation deeper. If you don't see how their proposed solutions will get them to the best possible outcome, follow up with more inquiry. What can you ask in that moment to help your team member connect with the core problem they're trying to solve?

One effective strategy is to go with a variation of Question 6: "How does that option get you to your best possible outcome?" If that doesn't get you there, keep going. Expect the conversation to go back and forth through a few iterations; typically, this is not a linear process. You might need to keep toggling among the three Aligning questions—prioritizing, brainstorming, and evaluating—until they reach clarity on their optimal solution.

DON'T SKIP THIS

Using the GR8 Coaching Framework, you empower your team member to use their whole brain, going as broad as possible and then as deep as possible to find their optimal solution, not just the obvious one. The first three GR8 Questions, the Aiming questions, get your team member going, focused, and real. They encourage that person to think about their situation and what they're trying to do. In these middle Aligning questions, we get serious, creative, and strategic.

Many of us simply wish to move directly from Aiming to Acting, skipping over this critically important Aligning phase of the coaching process. Maybe we can't fight the Ready, Fire, Aim habit. Maybe we give in to the need to play Expert Problem-Solver. Or maybe we don't take the time to get aligned because Aligning is where we invite creativity and innovation into our thinking—and creativity can get messy.

If you're the kind of person who races from point A to point B, take this moment to pause and commit as a Coach to moving through these questions with openness and curiosity. It's tempting to jump past or rush the Aligning phase and head straight for the finish line. The Aligning phase can sometimes feel too slow or messy to consider all the information. But rushing through is a surefire way to pick a suboptimal solution and maintain the status quo.

True alignment leads to better problem-solving and better outcomes. Does the solution always have to be wildly creative and innovative? No. If I'm brushing my teeth, I don't need to get creative. There's no route up through my foot that will somehow allow me to clean my teeth better. In cases like that, it's fine to do the same thing every day.

However, if I'm trying to figure out how to grow revenue or reduce expenses and risk for my organization, these are much more complex situations than brushing my teeth. In those instances, Ready, Fire, Aim rarely delivers the best possible outcome.

So, take time with the people you coach to ensure they're carefully thinking through their options. The more intentional you are here, the more successful you're likely to be later. (And if you'd like to take a deeper dive into the nuances of careful thinking, I have a whole chapter on the subject in *Ultra Leadership*.)

In the next chapter, we look at the final two questions in the GR8 Coaching Framework that will get your team member organized and going.

7

ACT

MAGINE YOU'RE IN A TEAM MEETING. TOWARD THE end, the Leader asks, almost as an afterthought, "Everybody knows what they're supposed to do, right?" It's a question, but it feels rhetorical, more like a statement. Everybody in the meeting nods their heads and drops off the call.

A moment later, one team member messages another and asks, only half-jokingly, "So, what exactly are we supposed to be doing again?"

Meetings like this happen all the time. They are almost always a total waste of time. They don't Align people. They don't Build bench strength. They don't Coordinate action. Lack of clarity about the plan to move forward and who owns certain outputs and outcomes isn't activating. It actually sets the team up for conflict, which eats away at people's engagement.

As a Leader, you're probably guilty of ending a meeting or two or three like this. I know I am. It's not that we mean to do it, but we're already thinking of the next thing on our to-do list, assuming everyone "got it," and forgetting to ask the questions that confirm alignment and establish accountability before the meeting breaks up and everyone rushes to their next meeting.

Unfortunately, while they may be innocent slip-ups, these oversights can lead to real problems. When no one knows what they're supposed to be doing—and they're too afraid or don't care enough to ask—nothing gets done. Deadlines are missed. Projects fail to get traction. And no one takes accountability for the lack of progress. That's no way to activate people.

This dynamic occurs in some coaching conversations as well. Using the GR8 Coaching Framework, you engage your team member to take Aim at their situation and determine their best possible outcome. You empower them to Align on the optimal solution for moving themselves and their situation forward. Finally, you activate them to organize their thinking into a clear plan and to secure a promise of accountability.

GR8 Coaches create alignment by leaving nothing unspoken. You must speak up and speak clearly. As thought leader Brené Brown likes to say, "Clear is kind."

At the end of a coaching session, you and your team member know what the plan is. The coaching isn't over until you know what's going to happen and when it will be completed.

That's what this chapter is all about: Acting. Now that you and your team member are Aligned on the best path forward to get them to their goal, it's time to secure a commitment to positive action. To facilitate that, you will ask the final two questions in the GR8 Coaching Framework:

- **Get organized:** What will you do?
- **Get going:** What's the simplest, best next step?

The purpose of the Acting phase is to facilitate Aligned action and accountability. As a Coach, the best way to create this accountability isn't by assigning work and due dates. It's by promoting engagement and ownership among your team members and encouraging them to clearly state what they will do and when they're going to do it. From there, all that's left to do is shake hands and let them get to work.

7. GET ORGANIZED
What Will You Do?

The GR8 Coaching Framework is a funnel-shaped process. Each question is designed to help your team members narrow their focus and direct their attention toward their most pressing issues. First, your team member surfaces an issue, then together you discuss barriers to solving those issues, essential outcomes for declaring success, and the best possible options to achieve that success. With Question 7, the conversation moves from theoretical to practical: "What's the plan to move toward that goal?"

Decision time. Here, the team member must organize their thinking, translate that thinking into an action plan, and then clearly articulate their immediate next steps.

Let's return to the example from the previous chapter. To recap, your team member's best possible outcome is to have a new sales leader onboarded by the end of the quarter. The best option they've identified is to promote from within the company in order to fill the role.

Your coaching now is to help your team member generate their plan of action. The question is pretty straightforward. "Okay, you want to hire from within and have the position filled by the end of the quarter. What will you do?"

In response, your team member should be able to list out a series of relevant steps:

- Identify a list of internal candidates qualified for the job.
- Reach out to the candidates and encourage them to apply.
- Determine who at the company will participate in the interview process.
- Set a decision date for hiring the right person.
- Establish an onboarding process and timeline to get the newly promoted employee up to speed.

Articulating a clear plan of action is crucial for ensuring follow-through and accountability. A well-defined plan outlines specific, attainable, measurable objectives with clear deadlines that activate your team member to achieve their best possible outcomes.

Coaching to organize a clear plan also establishes benchmarks for progress, making it easier to track performance and remind team members of their accountability for their contributions. This not only fosters a sense of responsibility and ownership but also encourages transparency and effective communication. By confirming the plan, you help your team member organize their thinking into actionable steps that keep them focused on their important work.

8. GET GOING

What's the Simplest, Best Next Step?

Assured your team member is organized, how do you help them get going? There are many instances where the plan can be complex. There may be a lot of moving pieces. The Get Going question provides focus. "There's a lot to do. What's the simplest, best next step you can take?"

This question is intended to complete the coaching session with a final, positive commitment to Act. The question is a reminder to your team member that they own their situation and their solution. Now, they need to Act.

As always, you can tailor your own follow-ups or variants to feel natural to you and suit your particular situation. Here are some of my favorite variations:

- "When you leave this meeting, what's the first thing you're going to do to Act on what we've discussed?"
- "That's a great plan. Now, what's the first step?"
- "If you only took one step today in order to move forward on this project, what would that be?"

Your team member should be able to answer any version of this question relatively quickly. The team member looking for a new sales lead, for instance, might look at the actions described in Question 7 and decide that the next best step is to alert HR that the hiring process is about to start.

Who Can Help?

As a supplement to the Get Going question, I often encourage the people I'm coaching to think not just about what they will do, but who they will do it with. To do that, I ask, "Whom do you need to engage for support?"

Often when we think about what needs to get done, we think only in terms of what we need to do. In reality, we nearly always have the freedom to enlist others in our mission as well. Sometimes, the answer is no one. Usually, the answer is someone. Sometimes, the answer is actually several people. Whatever the case, this question serves as an important reminder that no one has to go it alone.

This support can come in a variety of ways, such as the following, for instance:

- Your team member might want or need to delegate some of the work. In that case, the best next step might be for that person to reach out to another team member, describe their needs, and explain why that team member's skills and position will come in handy in the execution of the plan.

- Your team member might need your help to execute the plan. Perhaps they need you to have an important conversation with your boss—or another higher-up they wouldn't normally have access to—in order to open up a line of communication around this plan. In making that request, they have become empowered enough to use you, their team Leader and Coach, as a valuable resource.

Through the Get Organized and Get Going questions, you are establishing a contract with your team member. You activate them to engage, contribute, and achieve their best.

GR8 COACH CHECKPOINT:
TRUST THE PROCESS

Running in ultramarathons taught me the value of process. You have to respect the distance. No trail is the same as the last one. No race is the same as any other race. What is the same is the need to be prepared and follow your process for training and running. The best ultra runners have a process for training, for race-day preparation, and for dealing with changes and challenges on race day. You develop a process, and you trust the process.

Process can be our best friend when we are leading people and responsible for a team's performance. The GR8 Coaching Framework is a process that's been tested and proven over many miles and years. Whether you've never had a Coach's mindset, or you have always loved coaching as a way of leading, the GR8 Coaching Framework can elevate your leadership and your coaching skills—if you trust the process and practice.

You want to make the shift from Manager to Coach? What will you do? What's the simplest, best next step?

Here's a suggestion: Running fifty or a hundred miles takes practice. It's a lot of time on your feet on a trail. Similarly, becoming a GR8 Coach takes practice. I get better and hold myself accountable when I share my goals with another person. When I do, that person becomes my training and accountability partner.

- Find your training and accountability partner.
- Tell them you want to get better at coaching.
- Ask to practice with them.
- Find other people to coach.

From there, all that's left to do is hit the trail.

ENGAGE, EMPOWER, AND ACTIVATE

Using the GR8 Coaching Framework, you and your team member cocreate clarity around their important work. You're engaging them to get started, get focused, and get real about the opportunities and challenges impacting how they contribute to the team's shared goals. By empowering your team member to own their situation *and* their solution, you're developing their capacity to problem-solve and prioritize to get serious, creative, and strategic in order to generate a way forward. You're helping them organize their thinking into a clear plan with an identified simple, best next step, activating them and getting them going.

You resisted the urge to step in as Chief Doer and play Expert Problem-Solver. Because you decided to coach them, they remain in control of their own destiny. They grow in their ability to lead themselves. The goal is to serve the team and create leaders—people who understand the mission, own their role, and Act with intention.

The key to successful coaching is, once again, trust. You must trust that your team member has the capacity to succeed. They must trust that when you ask them questions, you do so in the spirit of concern and curiosity and a desire to help them accelerate their development and increase their ability to shape their work and activate to achieve their best. In this way, the coaching process generates even more trust. You trust they're activating on the right work in the right way with the right support. They trust themselves to deliver what they've planned. You trust they'll reach out if they hit a barrier and want some additional coaching. They trust you'll be available to coach them any time they want. That's the implicit agreement that emerges through the GR8 Coaching Framework: You and your team member strengthen your mutual trust.

TIME TO COACH

While we've spent the last three chapters looking at the GR8 Coaching Framework, I want to remind you again that coaching doesn't have to take a long time. When we practice coaching in our Be a GR8 Coach workshops, we give people fifteen minutes to move through the process. We do that intentionally to counter the mistaken belief that coaching takes too long. It doesn't.

Like our workshop participants, you'll find that you can coach anyone on anything in about fifteen minutes if you stick to the GR8 Coaching Framework. In fifteen minutes, you engage someone and empower them to Aim carefully, Align on the best way forward, and Act to achieve their best results. Some coaching conversations may be longer, but it's not because coaching takes a long time; it's because the situation warrants taking more time.

The GR8 Coaching Framework enables you to coach anyone open to being coached. It works with individuals. It also works to coach groups and teams. It can open a rich experience of collaborative inquiry for a group or team to take advantage of opportunities, solve problems, and cocreate a way forward to achieve shared goals.

Thus far, we've discussed the work of leadership, how to make the shift from Manager to Coach, and introduced the GR8 Coaching Framework. You're ready to coach. In the next chapter, we're going to look specifically at using coaching as a way of conducting 1:1s. Remember, the 1:1 isn't for the team leader, it's for the team member—the player on the field. Using the GR8 Coaching Framework as the foundation, we're going to turn your usual and ordinary 1:1 into a GR8 1:1.

8

THE LEADER AS COACH

N TRADITIONAL APPROACHES TO MANAGEMENT, PEO-
ple treat the organization as a machine that functions
most efficiently when it's hierarchical, with all decisions
flowing from the top down. Managers drive performance
and productivity by commanding their team members, controlling their effort, and expecting compliance.

As we discussed in Part One, that's the old way of doing
things. It produces results, but aside from being dehuman-
izing, it's also not particularly effective. The old approach
has a short shelf life. Being told what to do all the time is
disempowering, which leads people to disengage, doing just
enough to not get fired. When enough people are disengaged

because they feel disempowered, productivity drops, and the team and the organization become less effective. Remember, engagement isn't our default setting; people engage with their work and with the people they work with when you create the conditions that invite them to do just that.

The alternative approach I've espoused in *Ultra Leadership*, in *The Next Normal*, and in these pages calls us to push beyond the usual way of leading. Leadership still wants to drive performance and productivity. However, the leadership mindset and skill set that yield the best results have changed.

Following the way of Ultra Leadership, Leaders start with the belief that the organization is not a machine, but groups of people working together to realize a shared vision. In this environment, Leaders are responsible for creating the conditions that engage people, empower them to use their knowledge and skill to shape their work, and activate them to achieve their best results. Leaders help people engage with their work and with the people they work with.

THE 1:1 IS NOT FOR YOU

No one likes to be told what to do. We don't want to simply carry out orders. As Daniel Pink says in his book *Drive*, we all want a sense of autonomy, a chance to demonstrate our mastery, and a feeling of connection to a greater purpose. We know we can't get there on our own, so we're happy to receive coaching from others who've been there before us. A workplace that creates the conditions for those experiences requires a different kind of Leader.

One of the best ways to create those conditions is through carefully designed, coaching-focused 1:1s. In the old command-and-control world, the 1:1 was for the Manager. It was a time to tell employees what to do and then check up on them. Back in the day, it was a floor Manager walking up and down the assembly line, making sure that everyone did their little job at the right speed. When all work was in person, Managers used to feel like they were doing a great job because they got out of their office and walked the halls, stopping at cubicles to check in with employees. They were "managing by walking around." That made them feel confident that the people they were in charge of were doing what they were told.

Even if we wanted it to use it, we know that model doesn't work anymore. While the 1:1 used to be for the Manager, now it's for the team member, the player, the person who's doing the work. It's an opportunity to coach people so that they understand the highest intent of the team, shape their work accordingly, and activate to deliver their rolling ninety-day Tactical Action Plans.

In this Ultra Leadership model, there's still accountability, but it's no longer enforced through top-down commands and productivity audits. Instead, the 1:1 is more like an aid station in an ultramarathon, or a timeout in a basketball game, where the athlete can step to the side, refuel, talk through the situation with their Coach, and receive feedback so they can adjust and get back out there.

In this chapter, we'll tie together everything you've learned so far and apply it to the essential work of the 1:1. To do that, we will revisit and reapply the GR8 Coaching Framework to the context of the 1:1 so you can understand exactly how these conversations might play out as you shift to coach your team. I want you to start having GR8 1:1s. To do that, we need to get something straight right away.

NOT JUST A STATUS UPDATE

Too often, 1:1s are still simply status updates. Managers and employees meet every week or two, and the employee infodumps. This might make the Manager feel better about what's going on—and it gives them something to report to their own boss—but that information is rarely actionable. It just...is.

Imagine that you serve a team of twelve people. In the traditional weekly model, you're dedicating over a quarter of your workweek to 1:1s alone. If those meetings are always alignment- and action-oriented, great. However, if you're spending that much time just getting status updates, then there are better uses of everyone's time and much more efficient tools through which your team can provide those updates.

Your aim as a Leader is to design a team that does not need a traditional, usual, or ordinary management style.

You're building a team that is engaged and empowered to Act. The team knows what it needs to do and relies on you to call timeouts, give them some coaching, and get them back in the game. If you need more regular status updates, then arrange to get them. Just don't call them 1:1s.

KEY PRACTICES FOR A GR8 1:1

A GR8 1:1 centered on coaching the team member offers a more powerful lever than a status update. Here are two key practices to remember as you shift to coaching 1:1s.

Your Team Member Sets the Agenda

The 1:1 is for the team member, not you, so it makes sense for your team member to set the agenda for the 1:1. Most of us love having the trust and freedom to set our own agenda. When your team members know that the 1:1 is their meeting, they are empowered to get what they need from your time together.

This shift also frees you to think of each 1:1 coaching session as customizable to your team member's personality and current needs, rather than as a one-size-fits-all exercise in reports and status updates. When you reset 1:1s as coaching sessions, your agenda shifts. In the old model, your agenda was to take in your team member's status updates and instruct them on what to

> When you decide to coach for a change, your agenda is to help your team member succeed with their agenda.

do. When you decide to coach for a change, your agenda is to help your team member succeed with their agenda.

Your Team Member Sets the Cadence*

If everybody is working from the Team Roadmap and has a Tactical Action Plan laying out their work for the quarter, then you might not need to meet on the same cadence with each team member. It's one size fits one, not one size fits all.

When your team member is empowered to set the agenda, they are also empowered to suggest the cadence. Leaders who use the team management system we discussed in Chapter 1 create a culture of trust and accountability. The ninety-day Tactical Action Plan that each team member creates and executes becomes their promise of accountability. If the work is on track, some or all of them may need fewer 1:1s. When your team members are working from a solid TAP that you've signed off on, I encourage you to ask, "How frequently do you want to meet?"

Answers might range from continuing to meet every week to biweekly, monthly, or semiquarterly. People who are engaged, know what they need to get done, and are empowered to work through their own obstacles will likely prefer to keep making progress rather than adding meetings. If they need you, they know where to find you. Beyond that, you can stay out of their way. Individualizing the cadence frees up time for everyone.

GR8 COACH CHECKPOINT:
*CADENCE IS A NEGOTIATION

The cadence you settle on for each team member is a negotiation. If a team member wants too few meetings to enable you to feel connected and confident, negotiate a middle ground. As part of that negotiation, share your reasons for wanting more frequent meetings. And your reason can't be your anxiety. If you want more frequent 1:1s than your team member does, you may have some feedback for them that you've yet to share. Now's your chance.

If you have a team member who is constantly hitting their targets without the need for regular 1:1s, that's fantastic. But you might want to request a 1:1 with them at least once a quarter just to stay on the same page—and of course, to celebrate the fact that they're crushing all their goals. In other words, and whatever the context, find a number that will serve both of you. That number will rarely be zero, but it will also rarely be once a week. What cadence can you agree on that allows you to stay knowledgeable about progress but isn't intrusive?

Remember, it's rare for an engaged employee to refuse some level of coaching. By giving people more freedom, you foster more engagement and empower team members who are more willing to talk and use the time productively.

GR8 1:1s

With all that out of the way, let's look at the GR8 1:1s Framework. It's an adaption of the GR8 Coaching Framework, focused specifically on your team member's ninety-day Tactical Action Plan (TAP). Because these coaching conversations are specifically focused on the work your team member has articulated in their TAP, the Framework sequence and questions are constructed a little differently.

1. **Get Started: What's on track?** Hear about recent "wins" and recognize both effort and achievement. Grow your understanding of some positive aspects of individual and team performance.

2. **Get Real: Where are you stuck?** Explore what action or outcome on your team member's TAP isn't progressing the way they want.

3. **Get Focused: What's the best possible outcome?** Define near-term success.

4. **Get Serious: How might you be getting in your own way?** Gauge your team member's awareness about their situation. Deliver feedback if necessary.

5. Get Creative: What are your options for moving forward? Explore possibilities for taking action to get unstuck.

6. Get Strategic: How does each option get you closer to your best possible outcome? Get the person to look at the consequences of each option.

7. Get Organized: What are you going to do? Identify the best next steps.

8. Get Going: When are you going to do that by? Establish a promise of accountability.

9. Bonus: How can I help? Invite your team member to let you know what they need more of or less of from you to help them achieve their objectives.

Now that you understand the lay of the land, let's explore the questions themselves.

1. Get Started: "What's on Track?"

The Get Started question for the GR8 1:1 is a variation of the "What's going on?" question. Because you are focusing on the team member's TAP, the question is designed to open the conversation by inviting your team member to share their recent wins. This gives you the opportunity to grow your understanding of some positive aspects of their performance.

GR8 1:1s FRAMEWORK

1. **GET STARTED:** What's on track?

2. **GET REAL:** Where are you stuck?

3. **GET FOCUSED:** What's the best possible outcome?

4. **GET SERIOUS:** How might you be getting in your own way?

5. **GET CREATIVE:** What are your options for moving forward?

6. **GET STRATEGIC:** How does each option get you closer to your best possible outcome?

7. **GET ORGANIZED:** What are you going to do?

8. **GET GOING:** When are you going to do that by?

BONUS: How can I help?

Starting with wins also helps grow your understanding of how the individual works and how they're performing. As they share what's on track, they might tell you a story that gives you deeper insight into current dynamics.

I used to coach a CEO who told his team members, "Don't break your arm patting yourself on the back." He thought pausing to celebrate would detract his team from getting on with their work. I disagreed with him.

If anything, we don't pause to celebrate the accomplishments of our team members *enough* as they make progress on their TAPs. In our coaching workshops, I often ask the group to raise their hands if anyone there believes they receive *too much* positive feedback. I've never seen a single hand go up.

Like many people, this CEO had a mistaken belief that validation and reinforcement were superfluous. In reality, both are deeply human needs, whether we're five years old or fifty-five. As we age, we might get better at validating ourselves and functioning without as much external reinforcement, but it still feels good and moves the needle in a positive direction.

Even belated praise and celebrations feel good. Another of my coaching clients recently texted me a screenshot of a message he'd received from someone reminiscing about the strong team he'd built at his company ten years earlier. Receiving that validation felt so good that he also wanted to share it with me. Never mind that he's a high-ranking Leader at a Fortune 50 company who has achieved a great deal over his career. And never mind that he hadn't worked with the person who'd sent him the message in nearly a decade. This surprise praise still made this executive's day.

By asking "What's on track?" and celebrating your team member, you automatically increase engagement. When we receive compliments, we feel validated and valued, which in turn releases positive neurotransmitters in our brains, setting a productive baseline for whatever you talk about next.

2. Get Real: "Where Are You Stuck?"

Once you've celebrated some wins, it's time to get real and find out where your team member may be stuck. The second question in the GR8 1:1 is a variation of "What's in your way?" Because you're looking at your team member's TAP with them, the question becomes, "Where are you stuck?" Alternatively, you might reframe the question as "What isn't progressing in the way you might want it to?"

This question gets to the core of your team member's agenda for the conversation. Giving them a chance to discuss their obstacles is the first step in their finding the solution they're looking for. These sticking points could be anything— an unexpected snag in a project, challenges adopting a company-wide initiative, or a sour relationship with a colleague. The quicker you and your team member surface where they are stuck, the quicker they can get unstuck.

There may be times when your team members aren't stuck on anything. If they aren't experiencing any major obstacles, shift your focus to their development goals. What's on track there? How do they know? What are they learning? What are people noticing as they develop themselves?

3. Get Focused: "What's the Best Possible Outcome?"

Now that your team member has shared where they are stuck, your coaching helps them refocus on what success looks like. Just as you do when you use the GR8 Coaching Framework, you ask, "What's the best possible outcome?" Wherever they're stuck, there's an idea of what getting unstuck looks like. What is that?

Focusing on the best possible outcome before moving to action is a critical step in achieving success, as it sets a clear direction and aligns your team member's efforts with their ultimate goals. Research in the fields of psychology and goal-setting theory supports this assertion. By asking someone to envision the best possible outcome, you help them create a mental image that guides their actions, increases persistence, and improves decision-making. Additionally, research on *mental contrasting* by Gabriele Oettingen, a psychologist and professor at NYU and the University of Hamburg, shows that combining positive visualization with realistic planning (considering both the desired outcome and potential obstacles) leads to more effective goal pursuit.[40] This process of clarifying and focusing on the ideal outcome

---

40 Oettingen, G., "Expectancy effects on behavior depend on self-regulatory thought," *Social Cognition*, 18(2) (2000): 101-129, doi:10.1521/soco.2000.18.2.101.

before taking action ensures that your efforts are pur-
pose-driven and aligned with what you truly want to achieve.

4. Get Serious:
"How Might You Be Getting in Your Own Way?"

The Get Real question asks, "Where are you stuck?" What
your team member shares may surface external factors hindering their progress. A variation of a follow-up we can ask
in the GR8 Coaching Framework, the Get Serious question
invites your team member to reflect on how their beliefs or
behaviors may be contributing to their being stuck. Because
the purpose of the 1:1 is to engage, empower, and activate
your team member, the question is more pointed: "How
might you be getting in your own way?"

Remember, you're coaching the person here, not the
problem, and not all barriers are external. Some are internal.
With this question, you're encouraging your team member to
consider how their beliefs, behaviors, or habits are contributing factors in their lack of progress.

Not everyone has the self-awareness to recognize and
acknowledge how their beliefs, behaviors, or habits are holding them back. Maybe they have a self-limiting belief, an
unproductive behavior, an outdated value, or a gap in knowledge, skills, or experience that they're unable to recognize. By
getting serious with your team member, you create an opportunity to gauge their awareness both about their situation
and about themselves.

If your team member isn't aware of how they're contributing to their situation, ask if you can provide some feedback. Share what you are noticing. Your feedback should be about concrete, specific, observed, and recent actions or behaviors. Ask your team member to consider how this behavior or action impacts others. If they aren't able to or aren't sure, convey your reaction to their behavior or action. As their team Leader, you have a right and responsibility to share any expectation you may have about the need for them to shift their behavior and act in a different way. We'll go into delivering feedback in Chapter 9. For now, know that it can be a powerful part of the conversation that flows out of the question "How might you be getting in your own way?"

5. Get Creative:
"What Are Your Options for Moving Forward?"

Your team member is working to deliver the outcomes on their TAP. They're stuck on a couple of things. They've identified the best possible outcome for getting unstuck and back on track. It's time to get creative. Just like when you're coaching someone using the GR8 Coaching Framework, you want to spark creative thinking to get to the optimal solution and not just the obvious one.

To do that, ask, "What are your options for moving forward?" This question will get your team member to explore their options for getting their work back on track or accelerating their development of a particular skill or competency.

Creating space for creative thinking increases the likelihood that the course of action chosen is the optimal one, not just the obvious one.

Consider the story of the stuck truck that was in the news a few years ago. In a small town, there was a bridge known for its low clearance. One day, a large delivery truck tried to pass under the bridge but got stuck, wedged tightly between the bridge and the road. The driver tried to reverse, but the truck wouldn't budge. Soon, a crowd gathered, including engineers, mechanics, and local authorities. They suggested different solutions, including pulling the truck out with a tow truck, or even dismantling the bridge temporarily, but none seemed feasible.

Just as everyone was getting frustrated, a small child, who had been watching quietly, stepped forward and asked, "Why don't we just let some air out of the tires?" The child's simple suggestion was met with silence, followed by laughter. The professionals had overlooked the obvious in their rush to find a complex solution.

But then, an older mechanic who was also standing by thought for a moment and said, "The kid's right, but let's take it a step further. What if we let out just enough air to lower the truck a couple of inches, and then we gently reverse it out?"

They tried the approach suggested by the child and the mechanic. By letting out just enough air to free the truck and then reversing it slowly, they managed to dislodge the vehicle without damaging it or the bridge. The crowd cheered as the truck finally drove away.

The town officials later reflected on the incident, realizing that the simple and creative idea of letting out air—an approach no one initially considered—had provided the optimal solution. They decided to incorporate more creative problem-solving sessions in their future meetings, allowing space for unconventional ideas to surface before jumping to the most obvious solutions.

Creating space for creative thinking—like listening to the young child and the mechanic—can lead to more optimal solutions, rather than settling for the first, most apparent answer. There is value in taking a step back, considering different perspectives, and allowing time for creative ideas to emerge.

This is the meat of the coaching conversation—time and space for creative thinking. You've had a chance to give them feedback, and they've demonstrated some awareness about how they're contributing to their current state. Now you want them to lay out all the options for moving forward.

6. Get Strategic: "How Does Each Option Get You Closer to the Best Possible Outcome?"

Once your team member has thought expansively about their options, it's time to consider the implications of each one. To help them with that, ask, "How does each option get you closer to the best possible outcome?"

The Get Strategic question short-circuits the Ready, Fire, Aim tendency and builds the capacity for careful thinking. You help your team member examine each option, question their assumptions, and consider the implications of each potential course of action. Just as they own their situation, they own their solution as well. That's the whole point of coaching.

7. Get Organized: "What Are You Going to Do?"

As in the GR8 Coaching Framework, the Get Organized question prompts your team member to think through and articulate their plan.

"What are you going to do?" enables you and your team member to Coordinate action. (Remember your ABCs from Chapter 1.) You're Aligned on their outcomes. You've provided feedback that helps them grow and Builds bench strength. This question and the next promote action and accountability with a specific, actionable plan and timeline.

8. Get Going: "When Are You Going to Do That By?"

Questions 7 and 8 go hand in hand. You want to know what your team member is going to do *and* when they're going to do it. Setting the time frame is an important and overlooked part of communicating for accountability.

The International Coaching Federation's original Core Competencies called this "contracting for completion." It's an essential piece of coaching. By stating the plan out loud and with a timeline, people are much more likely to follow through. It's one thing to have an idea or goal. You may even consciously decide what action to take and when to act. Saying out loud what you're going to do and when you're going to do it greatly increases the likelihood you'll follow through. Setting regular appointments with an accountability partner increases the likelihood you'll follow through to near 100 percent. And guess what. As their Leader and Coach, you are an important accountability partner! Stating what and when becomes a promise of accountability. You're not done with your GR8 1:1 without this critical information.

9. Bonus: "How Can I Help?"

In the GR8 1:1s Framework, we finish with one of the most powerful coaching questions you can ask: "How can I help?" This direct question serves as an essential reminder to your team member that you're there as a resource.

> One of the most powerful coaching questions you can ask: "How can I help?"

A Leader in one of our programs once told me that he hated this question. He felt it was perfunctory rather than sincere. He thought it was akin to "Let me know if you need anything." Fair enough. If you're operating in a command-and-control mindset that doesn't prioritize alignment, then any offer of help *is* perfunctory. In such a situation, the Manager might not know how to help or was only offering help to seem kind. And the team member wouldn't know how to ask for it, since they haven't set a plan of action, and expressing a need for help may be a sign of weakness in such a culture.

The Leader I just mentioned felt very strongly about this. So, we engaged in some coaching to get clearer about the potential benefits. "I can see how that would be very frustrating for you," I said. "When you show up to lead your team, are you sharing with them what the highest intent is?"

"Of course," he said. "Everybody knows what we're trying to achieve and what our goals are for the quarter and year."

"Great," I replied. "And you're constantly coaching them on how they're doing and where they're stuck, giving them feedback and helping them figure out their best next step?"

He said yes, he did all of that.

So I said, "Well, how powerful would it be for your team members to know that you understand what they're working on, believe in their ability to achieve their outcomes, and are available as a resource to them any time they need you? Under those circumstances, what do you think the impact would be of asking how you can help?"

He said, "They probably would find it really supportive, important, and impactful."

"Exactly," I replied. "Your team needs to know you're there if they need you."

Because this Leader's old boss had never provided him with a safety net, he didn't feel like he needed to provide one for his team members. Rising through the ranks in a command-and-control culture, he had been treated like another cog in an assembly line, without a sense of the bigger picture or faith that his boss would back him up. Under those circumstances, of course the Bonus question "How can I help?" could be construed as disingenuous.

But this Leader wasn't a command-and-control Manager. He was a GR8 Coach in training. He gave his team members all the information they needed, he made sure everyone was aligned on their objectives, and he trusted them to get their work done with minimal supervision. In that context, his offer to help wouldn't be perfunctory. It would be welcome.

In truth, any question has the potential to feel perfunctory if it's not asked with intention. The impact depends on how you show up for the people you support. If you're operating in command-and-control mode, all the GR8 Coaching questions are meaningless. However, if asked with intention and in the spirit of creating alignment, these questions are astonishingly powerful.

For instance, when you ask, "How can I help?" with intention, you invite your team member to carefully consider their own needs in order to achieve their objectives. A way to reframe this question to bring even more focus to your team member's thinking may be to ask, "What do you need more of or less of from me in order to succeed in your role?"

A range of responses could emerge:

- "I need more coaching from you."
- "I need you to talk with the CFO about something because you and the CFO have a strong relationship."
- "Can you get somebody on that team to take a meeting with me?"

- "Can you help me engage with this person to work out this situation?"

Sometimes, the answer to the Bonus question is simply "Can you just check in with me in a week to make sure I followed through?" Sometimes support is that straightforward, just explicitly committing to serving as the accountability partner. I hear some version of that from my clients all the time: "I'm going to do these five things. At our next meeting, can you ask me if I did them?" Knowing they'll be asked motivates them to follow through.

I can certainly relate to the power of accountability. In one of my first experiences working with a Coach, I said, "I want to write a book." Then I caught myself, realizing I'd said it out loud.

"Cool, when am I going to see the first draft?" my Coach asked.

I committed to two months. Then, I went home and told my wife, "I just told somebody I was going to write a book and I was going to have a first draft in two months. Shoot."

Not even a year later, I released my first book, *The Hero's Journey*. A decade later, I released my fourth book, the book you're holding in your hands right now. In each instance, saying out loud to a coach or friend serving as an accountability partner, "I'm going to write this book by the end of this year," made it real and got me going. That's the power of commitment and accountability.

BOLDLY GO AND CONDUCT A GR8 1:1

Let's say your team member, Jim Kirk, comes to his 1:1. Not one to believe in a no-win scenario, Jim wants to make sure he's on track with his Q1 TAP.

TACTICAL ACTION PLAN

Name: James T. Kirk				Quarter: Q1
ACTIONS: (What must happen to achieve each Outcome?)				**MY OUTCOMES:** (What will you focus on delivering?)
Recruit (Advertise Position)	Interviews (by 28 Feb)	Decide, Offer, Hire (by 15 Mar)	Onboard & Map 1st 90 Days (01 Apr)	Business/People Objectives New Manager Onboard
Align Team on Roadmap (by 31 Jan)	Coach All Team Members To Create TAPs (by 28 Feb)	Set New Team Governance Cadence (huddles & 1:1s)	Lead Monthly Roadmap Reviews	Team Aligned
Align on Target Operating Model	Select Initial Use Cases	Move Analytics Resources Close to the Business	Develop Plan to Organize the Data Products and Services	New Analytics Target Operating Model Agreed & Operationl
Process Design (by 15 Feb)	Comms Plan (by 15 Mar)	New Process Training (by 31 Mar)	Adoption Support & Tracking	Migration to New UX Process Complete
Read Coaching for (a) Change	Reset all 1:1s to Use the GR8 1:1s Framework	Practice Coaching with Training Partner	Get Feedback on Listening & Inquiry Skills	MY DEVELOPMENT GOALS Be a Great Coach
Exercise 3x a Week	Create Space Between Meetings	Check in with Partner	5-Minutes of Meditation Each Day	Be More Resilient

After checking in on how he is, how his family is, and so on, you begin coaching.

You: This is your time. Let's look at your TAP. What's
   on track? (Get Started)

Jim: I've interviewed four people for the open role
   and have a meeting with the other interviewers
   to get their take before I make a decision. The
   team and I had a great meeting where we aligned
   on our Roadmap for the year. Once I reminded
   them of our mission, it was great to see the team
   step into a really productive conversation about
   outcomes. Because of the way we structured the
   conversation, they really feel a sense of ownership
   for the work ahead.

By inviting Jim to share his success stories, you learn more
about his strengths, what he is learning, and what he can
contribute in the future. You also gain a better qualitative
understanding of how the people you lead think and act to
achieve their results.

More importantly, you get an opportunity to recognize
his effort and achievement. You get the chance to say, "Great
work, Jim!"

You: Where are you stuck? (Get Real)

Jim: The operating model work is stalled. There's a
   person on another team who has been resistant about
   where we are headed with regard to the operating
   model. I'm at a loss as to how to engage him.

You: What's the best possible outcome there? (Get
    Focused)

Jim: I'm able to engage him, work through what's
    driving his resistance, and get him on board.

You: You know you can't change other people. You can
    only help them want to change. How might you be
    getting in your own way here?

Jim: I'm not sure. He's not receptive to my attempts
    to engage him. I've sent him a number of meeting
    invites and emails. He just doesn't respond. This has
    been going on for a couple of weeks.

You: Can I give you some feedback?

Jim: Please.

You: You say you want him to engage with you. A couple
    of weeks ago, I was in a meeting with the two of you
    and some others. He was making a point, and you
    pretty much shot him down. You did the same thing
    to one of your peers in our huddle just this week.
    You needed to drive home your point and be right in
    both cases. How do you imagine people react to that?

Jim: I guess they think I have a need to win the debate.

You: Would you want to engage and collaborate with
    someone who has to be right all the time?

Jim: I guess not.

You: Okay. So, part of resolving your issue around the
    operating model work may be to rethink how you
    engage and invite people to collaborate. You need to

engage this person and get him to collaborate with you to design and roll out this new operating model. What are your options for moving forward? (Get Creative)

Jim: I think the first thing I need to do is call or text him and tell him about the feedback you just gave me and see if it resonates with him. I should ask him to give me immediate feedback if he feels I'm repeating that behavior.

You: That's a great step. What else?

Jim: I think I need to align with him about design principles and outcomes and agree to a protocol and cadence for collaborating on this.

You: What changes, if any, might you make to your development plan to help you break the "win every conversation" habit?

Jim: I have "Be a GR8 Coach" as a development goal already. I think I need to ask my accountability partner to watch more closely and give me feedback when I stop listening and being curious in meetings.

You: Great. How does each option get you closer to your best possible outcome? (Get Strategic)

Jim: Well, one resets our working relationship. The other creates more alignment between us about what we're trying to achieve and how we go about doing that. And the change to my development plan helps me with both.

You: Super. So, what are you going to do, and when are you
    going to do that by? (Get Organized *and* Get Going)

Jim: I can send him a text and call him today to
    apologize if I've made it hard for him to want to
    engage with me. I will ask for a longer meeting to get
    aligned on the work. My accountability partner and
    I are meeting on Friday. I'll ask her to keep an eye on
    me for the next couple of weeks.

You: Terrific. How can I help?

Jim: If you see me shut someone down in our huddle,
    message me and I'll correct myself in real time. I
    appreciate your coaching and your feedback.

You: Alright. Anything else?

Jim: I'm set. If I need anything before my next 1:1, I'll let
    you know. Thanks.

Using the GR8 1:1s Framework keeps you in Coach mode.
Your positive assumption is that your team members have
the capacity to see their situation and find their own solutions for keeping their work on track. Your coaching helps
them think carefully and adjust how they're approaching
their work and their colleagues. Your coaching concludes as
your team members make a promise of accountability to take
clear action within an agreed timeframe. You didn't tell anyone what to do. You didn't solve anyone's problem for them.
Because you show up as a Coach, you engage, empower, and
activate your team members.

FROM PERFORMANCE REVIEW TO
CONTRIBUTION MANAGEMENT

Have I mentioned yet that I don't like performance reviews? Allow me to explain.

Performance Management is a system organizations use for monitoring and evaluating employee performance. It's one way you keep employees engaged and productive. However, annual performance reviews as part of a performance management system no longer suffice in the real-time business world.

A 2018 McKinsey Global Survey revealed what we've come to know: When it comes to performance management, it is often poorly executed and ineffective. The McKinsey research report calls for establishing a system that is fair for everyone on the team by linking performance goals to business priorities and creating a culture of regular coaching and feedback.[41]

As I just said, it's no secret that I don't like traditional performance reviews. They're backward-looking and far too infrequent—just once or twice a year in most organizations. If you wait six months or a year to give me feedback about something, it's not helpful. In fact, it's demoralizing to learn I

---

41 Sabrin Chowdhury, Elizabeth Hioe, and Bill Schaninger, "Harnessing the Power of Performance Management," McKinsey & Company, April 5, 2018, https://www.mckinsey.com/capabilities/people-and-organizational-performance/our-insights/harnessing-the-power-of-performance-management.

could have been approaching my work better since February when it's now December. It doesn't encourage greater performance, engage me, or make me feel empowered.

Once again, the research bears this out. Employees are eager for coaching and professional development opportunities, with 68 percent agreeing that ongoing coaching and feedback conversations have a positive impact on individual performance. When Managers prioritize regular feedback over occasional performance reviews, in other words, they see better outcomes for their company. And yet, fewer than 30 percent of Managers effectively coach and develop their employees. Maybe they've settled into an old command-and-control culture or are addicted to playing Expert Problem-Solver. As a result, at these organizations, only 15 percent report effective performance management, and just 30 percent report outperformance relative to competitors. In other words, companies could dramatically improve performance management simply by prioritizing coaching and feedback.[42]

The team management system, including the GR8 Frameworks outlined in this book, support precisely this kind of "serve to lead," coaching-forward organization: You Align your team around a shared Roadmap. Team members shape their work with a ninety-day Tactical Action Plan. You engage them as a Coach to empower them to make the best contribution they can.

---

42 Ibid.

The GR8 1:1s Framework doesn't just make for more productive 1:1s. It also dramatically diminishes the need for the annual performance review. Every GR8 1:1 is a real-time examination of progress against objectives, an exploration of any knowledge, skill, or experience gaps that are contributing to your team member's performance, and an opportunity to rethink and reset how they show up, get work done, and contribute to the organization.

GR8 1:1s shift the focus of performance management from the rearview mirror of the traditional performance review to the forward-looking practice of contribution management. The more you coach, the more the official HR-mandated annual performance review is just a formality. There are no surprises, because you and your team members have discussed their performance all year long in every 1:1, and they've made any necessary adjustments in real time. By shaping their work quarter by quarter, they set realistic, focused goals that Align with the team's shared outcomes. They engage in check-ins with you at a cadence that they set.

GR8 1:1s shift the focus of performance management from the rearview mirror of the traditional performance review to the forward-looking practice of contribution management.

By making the shift from Manager to Coach, you're also creating a more psychologically safe environment. You're not telling your team members what to do, and you're not making a list of mistakes to surprise them after the fact either.

Everything a traditional command-and-control Manager might say during the annual performance review will have already come up during the many coaching conversations you had throughout the year. Free from the dread of the annual dropping of feedback bombs, the team member is empowered to shape their work, focus their development, and make their unique contribution.

One Leader who I coach says the shift away from the performance review model has been life-changing. Throughout the year, she keeps a copy of every TAP her team members have produced—and which she and her team members have already discussed constantly as part of their ongoing coaching conversations. Because everyone has received regular guidance, coaching, and support, no one has had the chance to drift offtrack, making the annual reviews opportunities to celebrate the year and look ahead.

Examples like this show why the GR8 1:1s Framework, as part of the triad with Team Roadmaps and individual Tactical Action Plans, facilitate and accelerate your shift from Manager to Coach, creating a culture of trust and accountability. In the next chapter, we'll look at a few additional tools that can help you become a Great Coach. We'll also need to mention those instances when circumstances don't call for coaching.

9

THE GR8 COACH'S TOOLKIT

E'VE SPENT A GOOD DEAL OF TIME focusing on two important coaching frameworks to help you make the shift from Manager to Coach in order to engage, empower, and activate people. The GR8 Coaching Framework enables you to coach anyone, anytime, in almost any situation. The GR8 1:1s Framework supports your work as a Leader, enabling you to coach your team members to own their situation, find their own solutions to shape their work, grow themselves, and achieve their best.

These are the primary tools necessary to coach for change. Before we wrap up, I want to share some additional tools that I find useful to my coaching:

- **The Weather Check.** The Weather Check Coaching tool helps you gauge a team member's performance readiness and coach them to greater emotional self-management.

- **Coaching for Accountability.** The stories we tell ourselves can take us off the field of play. The Coaching for Accountability tool helps you coach someone to see they have agency and can change any situation.

- **Feedback to Boost Performance.** From time to time, you will have to give someone feedback about their performance. The Feedback to Boost Performance tool helps you engage your team member with specific, timely, actionable feedback to help them identify and practice positive ways of engaging and contributing to the team's shared goals.

With our agenda set, let's dive right in.

THE WEATHER CHECK

As we've mentioned, engagement isn't our default setting. People engage with their work and with trusted colleagues. Our mood can impact how we show up to work and engage with other people. Our emotions impact performance. Our emotions, like the weather, fluctuate. When our emotions fluctuate, our ability to engage and perform fluctuates.

We use the Weather Check Coaching tool to help people identify and more precisely articulate how they are feeling so they can manage their emotions more effectively in order to engage and perform at their peak. The more emotionally self-aware we are, the greater differentiation we can make in terms of recognizing and managing our emotions and moods. It takes emotional intelligence to think carefully, engage, and contribute to the team's shared goals.

When we become emotionally triggered or flooded, we become stuck in that moment until we can find our way back to the present. If we are angry or sad, we're not in the present. Anger is focused on the past. So is sadness. Something happened that upset us, and we can become stuck in that moment. If you've ever gotten mad when someone cut you off while driving, you may have experienced this. Maybe you were mad for the rest of your drive. Maybe you were mad for the rest of the day. Or maybe you were mad for only a few seconds.

Anxiety or worry is a projection into the future. There's a meeting or conversation you're worried about. You're spending time and energy thinking about it. You're not in the present. You're in an uncertain future that is making you anxious.

Those we are coaching need to be in the right mood for coaching. They need to be able to recognize their emotions and regulate how they respond to them, so they bring their full brain into decision-making and actions, and not just their emotions.

When we are young and still growing in our self-awareness, we may be limited in how we articulate how we are feeling. Indeed, when someone asks, "How are you feeling?" our range of responses about our emotional state may be limited to "glad, sad, mad, or bad." As we grow, it's helpful to be able to go beyond describing our mood as glad, sad, mad, or bad and be able to use more precise descriptors.

The Weather Check Coaching tool helps the person you are coaching to more precisely identify their emotional state in order to shift from reactivity, where the emotion is driving decision-making, to responsiveness, where the emotion is contained and relegated to passenger instead of driver of behavior.

As you can see in the graphic, different words describe different emotional states. If we're feeling grateful, hopeful, or appreciative, then the forecast is good—not a cloud in the sky. If we're feeling irritated, bothered, or judgmental, then the forecast calls for a chance of rain. Or, if we're feeling fearful, angry, or hostile, then batten down the hatches. A storm's blowing in.

All of these possible forecasts are valid because all emotions are valid. They're not good or bad. They just are. Whether you're feeling overwhelmed by a packed meeting schedule or overjoyed that your favorite sports team made the playoffs, the important thing for this exercise is that you're able to identify that feeling so that you can understand how it might impact your performance.

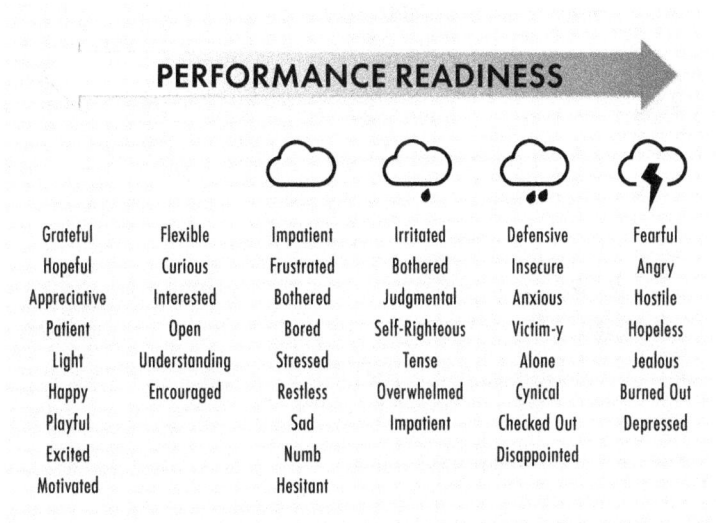

PERFORMANCE READINESS

Grateful	Flexible	Impatient	Irritated	Defensive	Fearful
Hopeful	Curious	Frustrated	Bothered	Insecure	Angry
Appreciative	Interested	Bothered	Judgmental	Anxious	Hostile
Patient	Open	Bored	Self-Righteous	Victim-y	Hopeless
Light	Understanding	Stressed	Tense	Alone	Jealous
Happy	Encouraged	Restless	Overwhelmed	Cynical	Burned Out
Playful		Sad	Impatient	Checked Out	Depressed
Excited		Numb		Disappointed	
Motivated		Hesitant			

Ultimately, that's what the Weather Check is designed to determine: performance readiness. If it's a sunny day, then you're ready to go. If there's a chance of rain, you might not be able to perform at your best, but you're okay overall. If a storm is on the horizon, then your ability to engage has been fundamentally interrupted. You've been emotionally hijacked. Nothing is getting done until the storm either clears or is contextualized.

Here's how it works.

How's the Weather?

1. Ask: "Which Word Best Describes Your Current State?"
Show the person the Weather Check visual and ask them to tell you which word describes their current state. This question shows the person you are coaching that you are conducting a Weather Check. Of all the possible responses to this question, the one answer that's not allowed is "fine." "Fine" doesn't tell us anything. We want to move past fine to a more accurate and authentic description.

Allow the person to describe how they are feeling and why. Maybe the person is frustrated because of their workload and the number of break-ins from another Leader in your organization. Your job isn't to make the person feel better. It's definitely not to play therapist. Your job is to help them stay as engaged, empowered, and activated as possible. But to do that, first you need to be aware of what's going on with them emotionally. From there, you can provide coaching as needed.

2. Ask: "How Would You Like Things to Be Different?"
This question is a variation of the Get Focused question "What's the best possible outcome?"

Maybe the person would like to feel more in control of their workload and better equipped to say "no" when possible.

3. Ask: "What's in Your Control?"
This question allows the person to identify and articulate what's in their control and lessen their level of frustration.

The goal is to enable them to see how and where they have agency.

Maybe they can review their commitments, compare their TAP with their calendar, and delegate or delete work that has crept onto their plate that is out of scope for them. Maybe they can practice saying "no" or negotiating requests more effectively with you or a colleague.

Remember, no matter how they're feeling, there's always a next step. Never are we completely helpless, floating in a sea of chaos.

4. Ask: "What's Your Next Step?"

You're helping the person see a way to sunnier weather. If they show up to a meeting and they're over in the rain clouds, that's legitimate. By identifying a next step, they are activating from a place of agency. Taking action is a way to find their way into the sun.

5. Ask: "Who Can Help You?"

This is always a great question, especially if our weather is on the cloudy or stormy side. It reminds us we aren't alone. There's probably someone who can help, if only in a small way.

Ways to Use the Weather Check Coaching Tool

The Weather Check is a highly versatile tool. You can use it for yourself during 1:1s, individual coaching sessions, and even during team meetings.

For Yourself

You can use the Weather Check for yourself. "Physician, heal thyself." After all, the only person you can change is yourself. Use the Weather Check to get better at naming how you're feeling and grow your capacity for emotional self-management.

In 1:1s

In a 1:1, use the Weather Check as a precursor or follow-up to the Get Started question ("What's going on?"), especially if the person seems upset, hijacked, or checked out. In cases where the person is experiencing serious storm clouds, you may want to or need to put the normal agenda aside entirely and focus solely on helping your team member perform a thorough Weather Check. After a while, your team members will become familiar with the Weather Check tool. When that happens, "How's the weather?" becomes an invitation to share an authentic response.

Sharing our accurate weather report can feel threatening if we aren't used to it. The more you use the Weather Check, the less threatening it becomes. Your team members come to understand that you aren't demanding that they disclose how they're feeling, but rather that you're trying to help them work through—or at least contextualize—those feelings. With the Weather Check as a guide, your team member can accurately locate their emotional weather without disclosing more than they're comfortable with or more than what's appropriate.

If someone comes into their 1:1 with an especially chipper, positive attitude, I might not formally use the Weather Check. Instead, I might say, "It seems your weather is full sunshine today—do I have that right?" The person can then confirm or clarify if needed.

In Team Meetings

The Weather Check is a great icebreaker or team-building conversation starter. The Weather Check offers an easy shorthand for developing emotional self-awareness and practicing appropriate self-disclosure.

Particularly if you haven't met as a group in a few weeks or even a whole quarter, try starting with a Weather Check. When I practice this with groups, I ask everyone to pick a word that describes their current state. Then, each person describes how they are feeling and what might be behind that. The description often surfaces nuances that they hadn't previously articulated. Then, if there's time, I'll invite the group to coach one another using the questions described earlier.

With frequent use, you and your team will become more attuned to your emotions and how they impact performance, which will in turn make you, your team, and the organization more productive.

Making space to talk about emotions and recenter personal agency quickly helps people to shift states. That doesn't mean you'll always move someone directly into full sun, but they'll see a way out of the clouds and a path to action.

As teams begin to make Weather Checks a regular routine, many will find ways to integrate them into their day-to-day. For instance, a Leader at one of our client organizations put a poster of the Weather Check Coaching tool on her office wall, so whenever anyone comes in, she can start by asking them about their weather.

COACHING FOR ACCOUNTABILITY:
UNDOING THE DRAMA TRIANGLE

Keeping people engaged, empowered, and activated means keeping them on the field of play. They're in the game. Keeping some team members on the field can be more challenging than others.

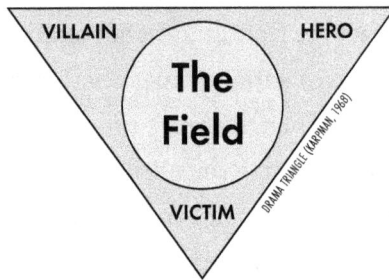

The Drama Triangle is a social model of human interaction first introduced by psychiatrist Stephen B. Karpman in 1968. The Drama Triangle helps us objectively examine how we describe our personal and professional relationships. The triangle maps a type of destructive interaction that can occur among people in conflict. Here's what the Drama Triangle looks like. I've added the circle in the center. That's the *field*. The field is where we want to be. We want to stay out of the corners.

Things happen that can trigger us emotionally and pull us off the field. When we get pulled off the field, we have to tell a story about why that happened. What does the experience mean? To make meaning of our experiences, we tell stories. Stories have characters like villains, victims, and rescuers (heroes). When we make someone else (or something else, like another team or some process) the villain in our story, we become the victim by default. We cannot lead if we cast ourselves as victims or play the hero and try to rescue people. When we cast ourselves as the victim in our own story, we take ourselves off the field of play. When that happens, we are likely to commit a foul of some kind. When we do that, we are likely to become the villain in someone else's story.

Let's look at an example. Say someone on your team has come to you with a story about an experience they had. They're venting about Rajiv in Finance, or the whole sales team, or an HR process they are having trouble with. That person, team, or process is the villain in their story.

- "Life would be great if only Rajiv hadn't acted that way in the meeting."
- "Life would be great if only the sales team was easier to work with."

- "Life would be great if only that HR process were easier to use."

Statements like these are a sure sign that your team member is in the victim corner. They're blaming someone, some group, or something for interfering with how they want things to be. They're hoping you'll agree with them and maybe even take action on their behalf. As soon as you do, you assume the role of hero.

We don't need another hero. This is an opportunity for you to lead. Leaders don't rescue; Leaders coach and empower people to own their reality and shape their way forward.

Leaders don't rescue; Leaders coach and empower people to own their reality and shape their way forward.

You're thinking, *Greg, how come you can't lead as a hero? Aren't heroes the good guys? Aren't they great Leaders?* Yes, heroes are the good guys, and great Leaders are often referred to as heroes. But in context of the Drama Triangle, at least, the concepts are at odds. Here are two reasons why.

First, when you try to play the hero, often you'll end up being recast as the villain in someone else's story. They didn't ask you to play the hero. They didn't ask you to fix anything. So why are you getting in their business? As Ultra Leaders, we need to learn to supportively back off.

Second, the impulse to play the hero is just another expression of the impulse to play the role of Chief Doer and

Expert Problem-Solver. We've spent a whole book talking about why that may not be the most productive approach. Enough said on that.

From Drama Triangle to
Coaching and Accountability Triangle

The Coaching for Accountability tool helps you avoid getting sucked into playing the hero in someone else's story. It helps you make the shift from hero to Coach so that someone else can shift from complainer or victim to owner. It helps you get the person back on the field. It helps you reframe the story from a drama story into a coaching and accountability story.

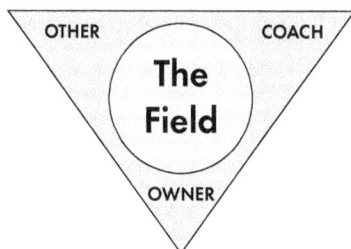

The Coaching and Accountability Triangle replaces the victim, villain, and hero roles with more productive ones: owner, other, and Coach. When you shift from hero to Coach, you help the person see that they have agency. You remind them that other people are not villains; they're simply people who are wired differently. From this perspective, it's easier to understand that 99 percent of the time, people aren't trying to upset each other. Sometimes things come out wrong in a conversation, or we're operating from a different set of priorities, but other people or teams or processes are not out to ruin anyone's life.

When you shift from hero to Coach, you help the person see that they have agency. You remind them that other people are not villains; they're simply people who are wired differently.

In fact, here's something I've learned along the way. I have never, in all my years working in organizations, met someone who casts themselves as the villain. No one does that. Even Logan Roy, who we talked about in Chapter 3 and who is the villain in almost everyone's story on *Succession*, isn't really a villain. He actually sees himself as a victim most of the time. That's why he's such a terrible Leader. He's a victim to what he perceives as the disloyal, incompetent, ineffective people around him.

Once we stop casting others as the villain in our story, we cease to play the victim, and we acknowledge our ownership over our circumstances.

Coaching for Accountability

Use the Coaching for Accountability tool to make the shift from hero to Coach so someone else can shift from victim to owner. When someone comes to you with what you determine to be a victim story, ask them if you can coach them about the situation and help them out of the corner and into a place of ownership and empowerment. Here's how.

"What Is Going On?" (Get Started)

- Ask: "Who or what is the villain?" Who or what is the villain in your team member's story? Is it a person? Is it a team? Is it a process that they find hard to use? Talk about who or what seems to be the villain.

- Ask: "What beliefs do you have about the situation, the people involved, or the process causing the situation from your perspective?" Explore your team member's underlying beliefs about the situation and the people involved. Does your team member think someone they work with is an evil, sadistic jerk who's trying to ruin their life, when they're just a colleague trying to do their best? This line of questioning helps you understand your team member's perspective.

- Ask: "What have you done about the situation so far?" It's good to check in and see if your team member has done anything to resolve this situation or prior situations. By asking this, you may stumble upon a pattern that is driving an ongoing story for your team member.

- Ask: "What has happened as a result of the actions you've taken or haven't taken?" This question opens an exploration of what your team member's prior actions or inaction resulted in for them. It can help them step into fuller ownership of their experience.

"What Is in Your Control?" (Get Real)

- Say: "From this moment on, you own how you think, feel, and respond to this situation. That's ownership." We can't control other people. We can't control a lot of what happens around us. We can control how we respond to others and to what happens around us. As the existential philosopher Viktor Frankl said in *Man's Search for Meaning*, "Everything can be taken from a man but one thing: the last of the human freedoms—to choose one's attitude in any given set of circumstances, to choose one's own way."

- Ask: "What do you want to do?" We each own how we think, feel, and respond to a situation. Reminded of their autonomy and ownership, what does your team member want to do about their situation? What are the options? Help them get creative to move into full ownership.

"What Will You Do?" (Get Organized)

- Ask: "What's the plan?"
- Ask: "Who needs to be consulted or informed?"
- Ask: "When will you take action?"

The options they identify could range from doing nothing to circling back with the other person or team about the issue. They might commit to a different way of engaging with a challenging team, learn how to use a difficult process more effectively, or advocate to change that process. Whatever or whomever the supposed villain is, when you decide to coach rather than rescue, you help your team member own their situation and take action to address it.

"What's the Best Next Step?" (Get Going)

Just like when you're using the GR8 Coaching Framework or conducting a GR8 1:1, you want to have your team member state their best next step. Saying it out loud makes it real.

A Very Brady Example

Imagine a member of your team, Jan, comes to you to complain about an upsetting comment Marcia made in a meeting. Jan has a story as to why Marcia said what she did—which likely isn't true. If you affirm Jan's narrative, you reinforce her status as victim and your stance as hero. Doing so might make both of you feel better, but it also keeps Jan stuck in the past instead of activated toward a productive future.

Further, once Jan has received validation for her perceived victimization, she'll likely continue to seek evidence that Marcia is a villain. The next time Marcia cuts her off or takes too much credit, Jan will likely say to herself, "See? What a jerk!" From there, Jan will crave even more validation. Maybe she'll text another team member to continue recruiting others to accept her "Marcia is a villain" narrative.

Instead of coaching Jan to assume positive intent and engage Marcia in a productive way to clear up a misunderstanding or misalignment, by assuming the hero role in Jan's story, you actually encourage her to relate to Marcia as a villain. When she does, she becomes the villain in Marcia's story. Then Marcia comes to you. You're now fully in the middle. You'll satisfy neither of them and become the villain in the next telling of their stories.

IT'S TIME FOR FEEDBACK

As promised in earlier chapters, here's a tool that helps you deliver feedback to boost performance. We just said that keeping some team members on the field and performing can be more challenging than others. Sometimes a team member may have performance issues like failing to communicate with stakeholders, failing to contribute in meetings, high turnaround times, missing deadlines, being uncooperative with peers or others, being resistant to change, or being unavailable during agreed-upon work hours.

Coaching in these situations can be more challenging. If you're like many of the Leaders who attend our Be a GR8 Coach programs, you may put off having these conversations. Raise your hand if you've ever put off a difficult conversation.

GR8 COACH CHECKPOINT:
ON BEING A VICTIM-FREE ZONE

Here's what I love about teaching people about the Drama Triangle: everybody gets it. In fact, most people can immediately see how they fall into this trap in their own lives.

Once you know about the Drama Triangle, you will catch yourself when you're telling yourself a victim story. I can't tell you how many times I've heard someone stop themselves midstory and say, "Oh! I sound like a victim," and then reframe the conversation.

To get the most value out of the Drama Triangle and the Coaching and Accountability Triangle, share these tools openly with your team—post them to relevant physical and digital spaces. Teams who know the drama triangle make a commitment to be a "victim-free zone" and call out victim language with one another. It becomes something they laugh about. A little venting is okay, but with a little self-awareness and intent, we can support and coach each other to make sure we remain in a place of ownership and empowerment.

I said this in an earlier chapter. It bears repeating: Never avoid hard conversations. If something is a minor issue, repair it. Minor issues become major issues over time.

A hard conversation now prevents a harder conversation later. Time doesn't fix anything, but it

A hard conversation now prevents a harder conversation later. can make problems compound. To wait, defer, or "hope" it will get better is not an option as both the organization's performance and the impact on coworkers start

to take hold and can have a compounding negative impact.

When you see a questionable behavior over time or see work products that don't meet expectations, talk about it— even if it's challenging. When you notice changes in performance or a lack of accountability, provide feedback and coaching as quickly and directly as possible to empower the person to own their situation and make agreed-upon changes to get their performance back on track.

Yes, having feedback conversations about performance issues can be emotionally charged. You will have to manage your emotions to design and convene these more difficult conversations.

A method we've all heard about over the years is the "sandwich method" of feedback. You tell the person something good that you like, then mention the difficult feedback, and then end by sharing one more bit of affirming feedback. This is not a great structure for feedback. When you intentionally bury negative feedback in between two bits of positive feedback, the critical point you really want to make becomes lost and fuzzy. You're trying to be nice, but in the process, you are likely creating more ambiguity. Most people can see right through it. They will label feedback of this nature as insincere and lacking in integrity.

Feedback should be specific, address a specific issue rather than the person, and invite a dialogue.

Feedback, especially challenging feedback, is best received in the context of a coaching conversation.

Feedback, especially challenging feedback, is best received in the context of a coaching conversation. How might you structure feedback within a coaching conversation?

Feedback to Boost Performance

The Feedback to Boost Performance process provides a structure that can help keep the conversation on track and emotions in check. To start, be clear about why you see a need to give the person feedback.

- **Get Started**: Either ask, "What's going on?" or share your perspective about the situation.

- **Get Focused**: Ask the person what they're trying to accomplish.

- **Get Real**: Ask the person about external barriers they may be experiencing.

- Ask them how they might be contributing to the situation.
- Seek permission to share your perspective. Ask, "Can I give you some feedback?"

When you ask, "Can I give you some feedback?," they may say, "No," or "Not right now." That's okay. Sometimes I've had a day, and I don't want any feedback. Maybe tomorrow. Anyway, if they're not receptive to feedback at this particular moment, let them know that you have some feedback for them that you don't want to put off. Agree on a day and time within the next twenty-four to seventy-two hours to continue the conversation.

S-I-S Feedback Process

Once your team member has agreed to receive feedback, follow the three-part S-I-S Feedback Process:

- The Situation
  - What prompted your desire to give feedback?
  - This should be a concrete, specific, observed, recent action.

- The Impact
  - Invite them to consider the impact.
  - Then share your reaction to the situation and how others reacted to the situation.

- The Shift
    - Share your expectations about a change in behavior or practice that would improve performance. (This is a flip on the "Get Serious" question: "What absolutely must happen?")
    - Ask the person if they have any questions.

If the feedback was well received, continue coaching using the GR8 Coaching Framework, asking questions 5–8.

If the person reacts poorly to the feedback, don't get reactive. Stay calm. Sit and be silent for a minute. Create space for them to calm themselves. If they aren't calming down, remind them of your intent. You are trying to help them boost their performance and make a more positive impact. If they still aren't settling down, suggest ending the meeting and reconvening the next day.

Finally, to wrap up the feedback conversation, return to the GR8 1:1s Framework:

- Get Organized: "What will you do?" This question is critical at the end of feedback. It's important to gauge how the feedback landed and if it is having the effect you want. Does the new awareness lead to an insight that sparks a change?

- The Bonus Question: "How can I help?" This question is of critical importance. As Leader and Coach to this person, you want to remind them that you are invested in them and available to help them as they take steps to address their situation and make any agreed-upon changes.

Dealing with individual performance issues is a challenging part of leading a team and critical to overall team performance. The more regular your coaching and feedback conversations, the more you create a culture of trust that helps people engage, feel empowered, and activate to perform at a high level.

WHEN COACHING ISN'T AN OPTION

We've covered a lot of ground here in Part Two. The GR8 Coaching Framework, the GR8 1:1s Framework, and the tools we've discussed here will help you make the shift from Manager to Coach. It's just about time to get out there and start coaching for a change. But before you do, there is one last point we should cover. It comes up in every cohort of our Be a GR8 Coach programs.

I strongly believe that coaching enables positive transformation and that making the shift from Manager to Coach is right for your team, your organization, and you. I also strongly believe that almost anyone in any situation can benefit from coaching. Almost.

As a Leader, you need to ensure that everyone on your team is accountable. Coaching is your first and most effective tool to that end. But if, after multiple attempts by you to coach them, someone isn't engaging, isn't demonstrating a sense of empowerment, and isn't activating to make their contribution, then you have to determine whether that person is the right fit for the role, the team, or even the organization.

Decisions like this are never easy, but it's essential for a team's success. There's a sociological principle called the Principle of Least Interest, which states that the person least invested in a situation has the greatest impact on the outcome. In other words, the person most unwilling to invest in themselves, their work, or their team will have the greatest impact on how that team performs.

The person most unwilling to invest in themselves, their work, or their team will have the greatest impact on how that team performs.

Research bears this out. On average, people who work near high performers show a 15 percent increase in productivity, while people who work near low performers show a 30 percent decrease in productivity.[43] As the saying goes, you are the average of the five people you spend the most time with. Ultimately, who do you want your team members to sit next to, Lisa Simpson or Bart Simpson?

Here are a few situations where coaching isn't the best option.

---

43 Dylan Minor and Michael Housman, "Sitting Near a High-Performer Can Make You Better at Your Job," *Kellogg Insight*, May 8, 2017, https://insight.kellogg.northwestern.edu/article/sitting-near-a-high-performer-can-make-you-better-at-your-job.

Clear Violations of Rules, Trust, or Decorum

If an individual has violated the law, behaved egregiously toward another person, or violated the core values of the company, that's not a coaching moment. It's a management moment. In situations that call into question both safety and legality, coaching is not the right tool. When people do something wrong, you need to level with them.

This isn't just for you and your team member, but for your whole team. The days of tolerating the "brilliant bastard" are numbered. In a coaching-forward organization, it's no longer acceptable for someone to be brilliant at their job and horrible to their teammates. GR8 Coaches do not tolerate brilliant bastards and all the drama that comes with them. If you do, you are signaling to your team that you value productivity over their individual well-being. And when your team members don't feel emotionally supported in their work, they won't be motivated to do their work.

How your team shows up reflects on you as a Leader. If someone continues to behave in a way that is contrary to the values of the organization or the team's working agreements and you fail to address it, the person ceases to be the problem. They're the symptom. The problem is you're not doing what you know you need to do. So, when you need to draw a boundary, do so swiftly and directly. A belief is something you have; a value is what you do.

GR8 COACHING CHECKPOINT: SEEK HELP

Sometimes people experience things in their lives that cause a variation in performance. We mentioned the Weather Check tool earlier. What do you do if someone is stuck in a storm?

Everyone has moments when circumstances overwhelm them, and they are compromised by their emotions. Normally, they are engaging, open to coaching and feedback. Something may be going on in their life at a given moment, when they're shutting down and behaving in ways that are out of character.

When you see that, you may need to engage your HR partner to discuss how to approach your team member with assistance in finding an appropriate outside resource like a therapist or social worker. By helping them find the help they need to address what's going on in their life, you can support them in doing the best they can as they work through it. Even though I've been a therapist, there have been multiple times where I've encouraged Leaders I was coaching to explore and consider engaging a therapist to discuss and work through some things that needed attention but were outside the scope of coaching.

The Uncoachable Team Member

Sometimes, you may invest considerable time coaching someone, and they just aren't responsive. They're not making the pivots you discuss when you offer feedback. What do you do?

In our Be a GR8 Coach programs, the number one issue Leaders want coaching on is how to deal with underperformers. They have a performance issue with a team member, and they've been avoiding dealing with it. They need a path forward to address it.

If you believe your team member has the knowledge, skill, and experience to succeed in the role, and a willingness to take feedback and be coached to change behaviors, keep coaching them.

Here are a couple of things to consider when faced with a team member who isn't responding well to coaching and feedback.

Your Time

When you coach someone, you're making an investment in them. You're investing your time and energy to help them feel empowered and activate them to contribute to the team's shared goals. You're helping them to develop as a person. If you start to recognize that your efforts aren't leading to results, then they may not be coachable. You have to ask yourself, *How much longer am I going to invest my time and energy in trying to coach this team member?*

I find this question to be especially revealing. In many cases when I ask Leaders how much longer they're going to invest in a particular team member, they respond, "I'm done." They have already decided the team member isn't a fit, isn't performing, and isn't responding to coaching and feedback. If this is the case, then don't give them six more months to flounder. You're done.

Once you've decided that all evidence suggests you have a team member who, in spite of your attempts to coach and provide feedback, isn't changing their behavior, you have a choice to make. If you aren't going to invest your time and energy in supporting their development any longer, you need to engage your HR partner and agree to a process to manage the person off your team.

Your Energy

On the other hand, if you do decide to give them more time—say 90 or 180 days—make sure you're ready to stay fully invested in their success for that time.

More importantly, clearly state what needs to happen. Say, "We've talked about your development goals. To succeed in this role, here are the behaviors I need to see from you."

Further, I suggest you say something similar to what I say to the people I coach. "I want to help you succeed, but I will not work harder than you do at your own development, your own career, and your own success. You own those. This is your experience, and you're responsible for your results."

You're not Sam carrying Frodo up the mountain. You're a Coach. You want and need coachable people on your team. Once you've decided someone isn't investing at least as much time and energy as you are in their own development and performance, the best possible outcome is to help them find a role, team, or organization where they can achieve their best. It's just not on your team.

An Emergency or a Crisis Arises

Coaching is not the best tool in an emergency or a crisis. If someone's about to step off the curb into traffic, don't pause to ask, "What do you think is the best option?" It's not a teachable moment. Yank them back onto the curb.

In an emergency or a crisis, be more declarative. Name the situation and give the directive. You're not coaching here. Instead, you're saying, "There's an emergency. Here's what we need to do. Let's get it done."

For example:

- A global pandemic hits, and you have to shift fifteen thousand employees from in-person to remote work in a week.
- During that pandemic, you need to quickly create capacity to process thousands of requests for PPP loans.
- An armed conflict erupts, and you need to shift resources and ensure your people in one of your geographies are safe.

These are all real challenges our clients have had to deal with. Because they built cultures of engaged and empowered people, there was no pushback when in the near term, to face real challenges, they shifted to a more directive style. It's what the situation called for.

COMPLETE YOUR GR8 COACHING TOOLKIT

We use tools to help us with our work. If you're building a table or cabinet, you need woodworking tools. You're building an engaged, empowered, and activated team that performs well individually and collectively. You need leadership, team-building, and coaching tools.

The tools we've discussed in this chapter are now part of your toolkit. Like the GR8 Coaching and GR8 1:1s Frameworks, they will help you in your work as you shift from Manager to Coach.

> **Want more resources?** Use the QR Code at the end of the book to find and download a copy of all frameworks and tools in the Coach's Toolkit.

SERVE TO LEAD

"SERVE TO LEAD" IS THE MOTTO AT THE ROYAL Military Academy Sandhurst in England. According to the *RMAS Anthology on Leadership*, "'Serve to Lead' is, of course, a paradox, but it is a paradox which must be understood by every officer cadet." It goes to conclude that "if cadets have not understood the meaning of the paradox, they have no business aspiring to be officers in the British Army."[44]

Nicolas George Taylor, writing for the *UK Defence Journal* in 2019, said, "Sandhurst doesn't necessarily teach, or prescribe officer cadets with the true meaning of leadership, but rather it places them into an environment with the tools for

---

44 Nicolas George Taylor, "Serve to Lead—Sandhurst and Its Tradition of Leadership," *UK Defence Journal*, August 1, 2019, https://ukdefencejournal.org.uk/serve-to-lead-sandhurst-and-its-tradition-of-leadership/.

officer cadets to develop their own understanding of leadership, one of which they may employ in their future careers in the Army."[45]

In these pages, we've talked about leadership in the same way. I've suggested a definition of leadership and some of the characteristics strong Leaders possess. I've shared frameworks and tools that can help you navigate and shape the environment in which you lead and a mechanism for developing your capacity to serve the team you lead as a Coach.

As I write this, though many organizations have either already adopted a coaching-based leadership model or are moving toward one, many others are still stuck in the old ways of command and control. I get it. Change is hard, especially in more mature, traditional, hierarchical organizations in highly regulated industries.

But just because change is hard, that doesn't mean it's impossible. Leadership isn't who you are; it's what you do.

Leadership isn't who you are; it's what you do. And you can always decide to change what you do.

And you can always decide to change what you do. I've tried to make the case that what you need to do is try coaching for a change to more effectively engage, empower, and activate people.

One of my favorite coaching clients is a senior leader in a large, well-established organization. He's a lifer: he came up in this organization and

---

45 Ibid.

has lived and breathed its command-and-control structure throughout his entire career.

When we first began working together, he was convinced this was the only approach to leadership that made any sense. He would tell his team what their work was, he'd tell them how to do it and when to get it done, and then, at the end of the year, he'd tell them how they did through their annual performance review. He treated his team like a machine to be run as efficiently as possible.

But his team wasn't running that efficiently, and he didn't understand why. So, I asked him a question: "What does success look like to your team?" As we unpacked that question together, he came to a stunning realization: his team didn't like him telling them what to do all the time. As his team was comprised of fairly senior leaders themselves, they wanted a voice in defining their own goals and objectives.

Armed with this new information, this Leader decided to try something radical, at least for him: let the team produce the first draft of their annual goals and quarterly Tactical Action Plans. This meant less work for him and more engagement and accountability for his team. Instead of trying to convince them of what to do, they were already on board because— shocker—it was their idea! They defined their work in alignment with the organizational vision and the team's mission and shared goals, shaped how they would deliver what was theirs, and owned their experience and results. And then, after he had a chance to provide his own input, they executed it.

For this senior Leader, the experience was a real eye-opener. Never in his wildest dreams did he think that, by ceding control, working less, and inviting input, his team would be more engaged and effective than ever. Best of all, he now had more time in his day to pursue other high-impact work.

If this dyed-in-the-wool disciple of the old command-and-control model could learn some new tricks, so can you. Anyone can learn to become a GR8 Coach. All it takes is a little commitment and accountability—and, of course, a useful framework to light your path. As this book winds down and you get ready to apply these lessons in the real world, here are a few final things to keep in mind.

TRUST IS TABLE STAKES

Trust is table stakes. Without it, there's no game. The three most powerful words a Leader can say to a team member are "I trust you." When we try coaching for a change, when we show up as Coaches, we communicate our trust not just through our words but also through our actions. Trust becomes implicit in that process.

To communicate trust, we must let go of our urge to be Chief Doer and Expert Problem-Solver. Telling people what to do is just another way of saying, "I don't trust you." Worse, it creates a negative cycle. When you dictate an inflexible plan for what "needs" to get done, you're less likely to believe that another person could fulfill that plan. Your standards create an unimaginative, restrictive environment for you as well as your team members.

Let go of that need to control. Nothing will ever be 100 percent the way you would have done it on your own, but it's going to get done. The benefits to your working relationships will far exceed any trade-offs in a plan that diverges from your original vision.

When you resist the temptation to control and instead empower others to do their work, you get to see how another competent team member would approach a problem. You'll inevitably learn something by observing their work. You may even be pleasantly surprised by how well they achieve a goal. In that rewarding process, they teach you something, and you can now productively rethink your own approach to similar projects. You're listening with full attention and empathy, and you're open to being changed. When you extend trust, you are serving to lead.

As a Leader and a Coach, you serve your team by creating the conditions for them to succeed. To do that, remember your ABCs and count to three. When you Align people, you serve them. When you Build bench strength, you serve people. When you Coordinate action, that's serving people. Team Roadmaps articulate your guiding stars and empower your team to shape their work using individual Tactical Action Plans and making aligned decisions on their own.

> As a Leader and a Coach, you serve your team by creating the conditions for them to succeed.

You're building a team that requires a Coach, not a Manager, let alone a Micromanager. You serve your team when you coach and empower them to create the experience and results that represent success to the organization and the team. Helping the team engage their work and one another, helping them operate, is a way to serve the team you lead. Follow the recipe and you will have engaged, empowered, and activated your team.

CULTIVATE ENGAGEMENT, EMPOWERMENT, AND ACTIVATION

The people on your team don't engage the organization. They engage their work and other people, including you. Cultivating engagement requires you to be profoundly present to team members and care about them as individual humans as well as direct reports. Being present to and deeply observant of your team members makes it easier for them to work with you and respond to you as an individual as well.

You serve the team, not the other way around.

Remember, they work with you, not for you. You serve the team, not the other way around.

Before any interaction with your team members, ask yourself, *Am I showing up in a way that encourages people to engage with me? Am I empowering them enough for them to feel engaged?*

A disempowered team is a dependent team, one in which you, the Leader, remain the Chief Doer and Expert

Problem-Solver who dictates all the answers. That's not the kind of culture an Ultra Leader and GR8 Coach creates. An empowered team knows how to solve problems as they arise on their own. They approach challenges and find solutions independently. They own their work and their solutions.

Embracing the paradox of "serve to lead," your job isn't to carry your team from A to B, but to help them figure out how to get from A to B by themselves. You are coaching to lead. To do this, use the GR8 Coaching Framework:

1. Get Started by asking, "What's going on?"
2. Get Focused by asking, "What's the best possible outcome?"
3. Get Real by asking, "What's in your way?"
4. Get Serious by asking, "What absolutely must happen?"
5. Get Creative by asking, "What are your options?"
6. Get Strategic by asking, "How does each option get you closer to your best possible outcome?"
7. Get Organized by asking, "What will you do?"
8. Get Going by asking, "What's the simplest, best next step?"

When you coach to lead, you are doing the following:

- **Aligning people**, reinforcing the team's mission, highest intent, and outcomes and each person's contribution.

- **Building bench strength**, providing coaching, feedback, and guidance as each team member works to grow their capacity to succeed in their current role and maintain pace to step into the next.
- **Coordinating action**, ensuring people are focused on their important work so that there are no gaps or duplication of effort as the team works to achieve its shared goals.

When you coach to lead, you are doing these things:

- **Engaging people**, extending trust and being present in an empathetic way that maintains a strong connection with you, their work, and their colleagues.
- **Empowering people** to own their work, their solutions, and their development.
- **Activating people**, inviting them to bring their best selves to their work.

CONTROL WHAT YOU CAN, AND LET GO OF THE REST

I recently had a coaching conversation with a senior Leader who was experiencing frustration. She was frustrated that while she wanted to shift from Manager to Coach, her organization was still operating in command-and-control mode. She was frustrated by her Manager micromanaging her. She was serving her Manager; he was not serving her. The organizational culture wasn't supportive of the leadership shift she was working to make.

We've all been in situations like this. Maybe it's your current experience. It's not fun. In fact, it's the kind of environment that compels us to dust off our résumés and start looking for greener pastures.

To be clear, the challenges this Leader faced were real. But she still had agency. Her Manager was teaching her how not to show up. Her organization's culture was helping her realize that she wanted to create a different experience for those she served as Leader.

We decided that the best course of action was to control what she could and let go of the rest. We discussed her best possible outcome and options for achieving that. While she was not in a position to shift the organizational culture or change her Manager, she was able to stay on course, make the shift from Manager to Coach, and create a team culture that engaged and empowered people.

As Leaders in an organization, we don't exist in a vacuum. We are being led as we lead. While tensions can sometimes arise, we always have the power to break the cycle of poor leadership. Just because the monkey above you on the ladder punched down on you, it doesn't mean you need to follow suit. *You* can create an environment where the team you lead is engaged, empowered, and activated. *You* can create a team of people who own their work and their outcomes. *You* can Align your people, Build bench strength, and Coordinate action. *You* can serve to lead. You can become a GR8 Coach.

You can become a GR8 Coach. And you don't need to wait for permission from anyone to do it.

And you don't need to wait for permission from anyone to do it.

THE END OF THE BEGINNING

You've reached the end of the beginning. The thesis of this book is simple: The old command-and-control models don't work. To be sure, they still exist. You may work in such an organization. Time is running out for organizations that refuse to break up with the command-and-control, "tell people what to do" way of leading. To succeed as a Leader in the modern world and create positive transformation for your organization, I want you to try coaching for a change.

As you take your first steps into your new identity as a Coach and begin applying the GR8 Coaching Framework to your interactions with your team, it might feel clunky. That's natural—but don't worry, it gets easier. I promise. Use these questions to break your own Ready, Fire, Aim habit of being Chief Doer and Expert Problem-Solver, and then allow yourself to continue to grow.

As you work to rethink, reset, and renew how you lead by coaching, I encourage you to apply the three modes of learning.

- **Think about it.** Always be evaluating how you show up as a Leader and the ways in which you might improve. Get in the habit of coaching as much as you can and then reflecting on how it went. Consider how you might grow your capacity to coach over the next three months. Ask yourself, What do I expect from my progression toward being a Coach?

- **Talk about it.** The best Coaches I know have Coaches themselves, even if just an informal one. The same is true for the best Leaders I've encountered. Find someone to be an accountability partner as you work to become a better Coach. A partner who can help you in your development as a Coach will add external, constructive reinforcement to your own work.

- **Test it.** It's unrealistic to think that you can just read this book, put it down, and immediately demonstrate mastery. We learn by doing. You're not going to get it right every day, but every missed chance is a potential opportunity for growth.

Your goal after putting this book down is to begin to show up as a Coach for a change, in order to create positive change. You have thought about it in the process of reading this book. Now, with whom will you talk about it? Where will you test it and practice it?

In other words, what's your ninety-day plan? Over the next ninety days, will you have practiced coaching whenever and wherever and with whomever you can? Will you have engaged an accountability partner? Will you have practiced conducting 1:1s using the GR8 1:1s Framework laid out in this book?

Set that ninety-day plan for yourself, marking where you expect to be in terms of your coaching abilities, particularly the changes you've made in your interactions with team members. Focus your plan on developing a coaching mindset, developing the coaching skill set, and utilizing the tools that will transform you into a GR8 Coach whose goal is to engage, empower, and activate people rather than manage and direct them.

And if you run into a few roadblocks? Keep at it.

I trust you have the capacity to change and grow.

I trust you can make the shift from Manager to Coach.

I trust that as you try coaching for a change, you'll become the Leader your team is waiting for.

I trust you can serve to lead—and to serve, be a GR8 Coach.

RESOURCES

All the tools, templates, and frameworks we've discussed are waiting for you. Scan the QR code to download everything you need to start coaching for a change.

STAY IN TOUCH

I want to hear from you about your progress on this journey. Feel free to contact me by email at *hello@ultraleadership.com*. Find us on the web at *ultraleadership.com* and *greggiuliano.com*.

Coaching

To accelerate your becoming a GR8 Coach, you may want to consider engaging an executive coach. Executive Coaching is a personalized 1:1 experience of leadership development. Contact us to connect with a Coach to support your ongoing development.

Be a GR8 Coach Leadership Development Program

The Be a GR8 Coach program is an immediately applicable learning and development experience with strong and sustained involvement of Leaders in the learning process. Be a GR8 Coach is a hybrid in-person and virtual leadership development experience commencing with a two-day in-person workshop experience and including individual and group fieldwork and Coach-led small group sessions.

Contact us to explore bringing Be a GR8 Coach to your team or organization.

Thanks for reading!

ACKNOWLEDGMENTS

My name may be on the cover, but this book only exists because of the contributions of many talented and generous people.

I'm one of the lucky ones; I get to do what I love. Being a Coach is a privilege. I am grateful to all the Leaders who have trusted me over the years to serve as their Coach. I have learned more than I can say.

I have been fortunate to work with many amazing coaching and consulting professionals in my career. I'm still learning from them and trying to pay forward the gifts of wisdom they share.

My family is a constant source of encouragement and support. I'm grateful that we laugh a lot as we find our way together.

I am surrounded and made better by our amazing team at GA | Ultra Leadership and all our delivery partners. Sina holds us all together. Kim selflessly just gets stuff done and keeps the lights on. Bridget Whitaker classes up the joint and makes everything look awesome, from our websites to all our collateral. Hussein Al-Baiaty and his team at Rising Authors focus and amplify our messaging, growing our YouTube community of Leaders.

Chas Hoppe at Cape and Cowl Media has been an amazing thinking and writing partner. If you're thinking you have a book in you, call Chas. Kacy Wren and her team at Wren House Press, including Michael Nagin, who designed our cover, and Sheila Trask and Tara Taylor, whose editorial assistance made this a better book, are a joy to work with. Without these amazing people, this book would have remained an interesting idea swirling in my head.

Lastly, I am grateful to the wonderful and generous Coaches who have engaged, empowered, and activated me on my lifelong journey of personal and professional growth, especially Duke. I hope I am doing you all proud.

ABOUT THE AUTHOR

Dr. Greg Giuliano is an advisor and executive Coach to senior executives and teams all over the world, designing change leadership and team development strategies to lead organizational transformation. His mission is to help Leaders and teams grow their capacity to enable positive disruption for markets, organizations, teams, and individuals.

Greg is the author of two #1 Amazon Bestsellers—*The Next Normal: Transform Your Leadership, Your Team, and Your Organization* (2022) and *Ultra Leadership: Go Beyond Usual and Ordinary to Engage Others and Lead Real Change* (2016), as well as *The Hero's Journey: Toward a More Authentic Leadership* (2014). Greg also hosts the *Ultra Leadership* podcast, connecting with real Leaders sharing real lessons for real learning.

Greg is the founder of GA | Ultra Leadership, a consultancy that works with Leaders and teams who want to go beyond usual and ordinary to engage, empower, and activate people and teams to shape the future consciously and confidently.

GA | Ultra Leadership focuses its work in three intersecting areas: advising and coaching Leaders to create strategic and cultural alignment, developing top team and leadership effectiveness, and building individual and collective capacity for organizational transformation.

Greg holds a doctorate in psychology from Alliant International University. He received his BA and MA degrees from the University of San Diego.

He is available for keynotes, executive coaching and team development, organizational change consultation, and high-potential leadership development.

For information about speaking, coaching, workshops, or booking Greg as a guest on your podcast, reach out at *hello@ ultraleadership.com.*

www.ingramcontent.com/pod-product-compliance
Lightning Source LLC
Chambersburg PA
CBHW071334210326
41597CB00015B/1445